The Organized Teacher

The Organized Teacher

A Hands-On Guide to Setting Up
and Running a Terrific Classroom

Steve Springer, Brandy Alexander, and Kimberly Persiani-Becker, Ed.D.

Illustrated by Steve Springer and Brandy Alexander

McGraw-Hill

New York   Chicago   San Francisco   Lisbon   London   Madrid   Mexico City
Milan   New Delhi   San Juan   Seoul   Singapore   Sydney   Toronto

1 2 3 4 5 6 7 8 9 0   QPD/QPD   0 9 8 7 6 5

ISBN 0-07-145707-0
Library of Congress control number 2005046307

Interior design by Pamela Juárez
Interior illustrations copyright © Steve Springer and Brandy Alexander

McGraw-Hill books are available at special quantity discounts to use as premiums and
sales promotions, or for use in corporate training programs. For more information, please
write to the Director of Special Sales, Professional Publishing, McGraw-Hill, Two Penn
Plaza, New York, NY 10121-2298. Or contact your local bookstore.

This book is printed on acid-free paper.

Contents

Foreword

At a time when teachers are overwhelmed with standards-based curricula, high-stakes testing, the pressures and responsibilities of accountability issues, and the everyday tasks of teaching, it's a wonder that teachers are as committed and determined to make a difference as they are. This is no truer than when walking into the classrooms of Steve Springer and Brandy Alexander at Lenicia B. Weemes Elementary School in Los Angeles, California. On any given day, you can walk in to their classrooms and observe a variety of activities from center rotations, felt storyboards, and hands-on projects. Students are helping one another, stories are being read on the rug, the teacher's aide is reading with small groups, and the teacher is working one-on-one with students.

In January of 2004, I had the pleasure of supervising student teachers from California State University, Los Angeles, during the Directed Teaching portion of their credential program. Two of my student teachers were placed at Weemes under the guidance of Steve Springer and Brandy Alexander. My first stop was Steve's first-grade class. Upon entering, I could immediately sense that the children had ownership of the room. Students' artwork was posted, their newest writing was securely in place next to the corresponding rubric, the children were talking to one another, and learning was obviously occurring. I couldn't have asked for a better place in which to watch the professional growth of my student teacher.

The next stop was Brandy's room. I felt as though I went from one exceptional venue to another identical one. I could hardly believe that my student teachers were being placed in such extraordinarily positive circumstances during a time that is often scary and unfamiliar. Steve and Brandy each offered a classroom where not only the students thrived, but so did the student teachers who were placed under their guidance for ten weeks.

Toward the end of the winter quarter, as the student teachers finished their final observations, I noticed a three-ring binder full of unique ideas from lesson planning to bulletin-board ideas to classroom discipline procedures. When questioned, my student teachers admitted that Steve and Brandy had provided them with these materials. I immediately asked Steve and Brandy why they hadn't published such materials for all new and existing teachers. From that time on, the preparation of this book was in motion. The three of us worked diligently for several months to pull together the makings of a practical, no-nonsense book full of blackline masters and usable resources.

Steve Springer and Brandy Alexander are dedicated teachers who show up each day with a smile on their faces and who have a classroom prepared for all learners and materials available for each child to succeed. I am honored to have had the opportunity to coauthor and advise for this amazing book and hope that new and existing teachers will benefit from our years of experience.

The most rewarding career is that of a teacher. While there are many aspects of the job that are less than desirable, the hugs, the smiles, the shared snacks, and the constant love from the children make up for any of the frustrating parts of the job. Having a classroom that has been carefully planned, organized, and maintained allows for more of the hugs, smiles, snacks, and love that will be generously showered upon you given the right circumstances. It is our hope that you will have your classroom management in place at the beginning of your school year so that you too can enjoy the rewards of teaching.

—*Kimberly Persiani-Becker*
Assistant Professor
California State University, Los Angeles

Acknowledgments

Teaching is a privilege. Parents and guardians entrust their children to you for the most alert hours of the day. It is an awesome task with great rewards. I consider it the most challenging job one could ever have. You face new experiences and challenges daily, and there is never a dull moment.

Today, as teachers, you are under tremendous pressure to continually raise the bar and reach for higher standards. It can be overwhelming and exciting, but I believe it is what you make it. This book is designed to offer you effective, practical suggestions to many of the daily challenges that you will face. The illustrations and checklist setups are easy to follow and a fresh break from the text-rich books that one rarely has the time to go through. We tried to cut to the chase in this book.

As a teacher, my time is limited; when I need answers, I need them quickly. I hope that this book can offer you real solutions and answers to everyday questions. I do want to add that these are practices that have worked for us. Every school, classroom, and teacher is different. These ideas have worked in my classroom—try them. If you like them, keep them. If they don't work, I hope they open your eyes to creative alternatives that will work for you. Let this book give you permission to enjoy the experience of teaching and the freedom to be creative in your classroom environment.

My first experiences with teaching were private swimming lessons and coaching. I remember one day observing another coach with his students. He was alive. He was having the time of his life and so were his students. I always think about him when I am in the classroom. I try to give myself permission to enjoy what I do. We are the adults, and we create our classroom reality. Teaching is an awesome gift.

I would like to thank all those individuals who believed in this process, those who saw the potential in all the materials that we have created over the years. I thank my mother, Donna Springer, a former kindergarten teacher herself, for all her support and belief in me and my potential to do anything I chose to do in life. I thank my family and friends for their unconditional support and patience during the creation of this book. It was an amazing process. My greatest hope is that it truly makes a difference in the lives of the people that I have the most respect for, my fellow teachers and educators.

—*Steve Springer*

Coming from a family where my mother, father, and grandfather are all teachers, I grew up having a great respect for all who choose to teach. When designing this book, we wanted it to be an asset to all teachers and their classrooms, and we hope that you will agree. This book was borne out of a need to create a resource that, whether you are a new or an experienced teacher, would spark fresh ideas, challenge your creativity, and push you to be the best teacher you can be. After all, the students of the world are depending on you! At the end of the day, you can rest knowing that you had a hand in everything happening in the world—from the dentists to the astronauts, *all* of them have had a teacher!

If you are reading this, you are probably a teacher, related to a teacher, or in close proximity to a teacher. If you are indeed one of these people, I would like to take a moment to say thanks. The job of educating students is an extremely important profession. Whether you are directly or indirectly involved in educating minds, thank you. Thank you, teachers of the world, for dedicating your life to educating the children of the world. (You probably learned a few things as well!)

I would like to thank my family and friends for their support during the creation of this book. Thank you to my mother, Candace, who reminded me during nearly every conversation my first two years of college that teaching would be a "noble"

profession. I guess I was listening. Thanks to my father, Larry, for providing me with a very sound model of what a "great" teacher really is. Thanks to my brothers, Brian, Brock, and Brason, for their support even though they still wonder how a boy who once duct-taped a rake to a motorcycle to rake the lawn faster ever got a job teaching. Thanks to Kashala for pointing out all of my spelling and grammar errors—and then bursting into charitable laughter. Thanks to Steve and Kimberly for being great partners in a project that will be an incredible tool for teachers and soon-to-be teachers. I enjoyed every minute of the process!

—*Brandy Alexander*

Finally, we both would like to give a special thanks to Annette Kessler, principal of L. B. Weemes Elementary School, for hiring us as new teachers. She saw our creative potential and has supported it over the years.

School Overview

The following is a breakdown of all the possible members of a school community. Get to know everyone on your school site. Every member of this community plays an important role in your success and the success of your students. Schools vary depending on the site and the number of students enrolled.

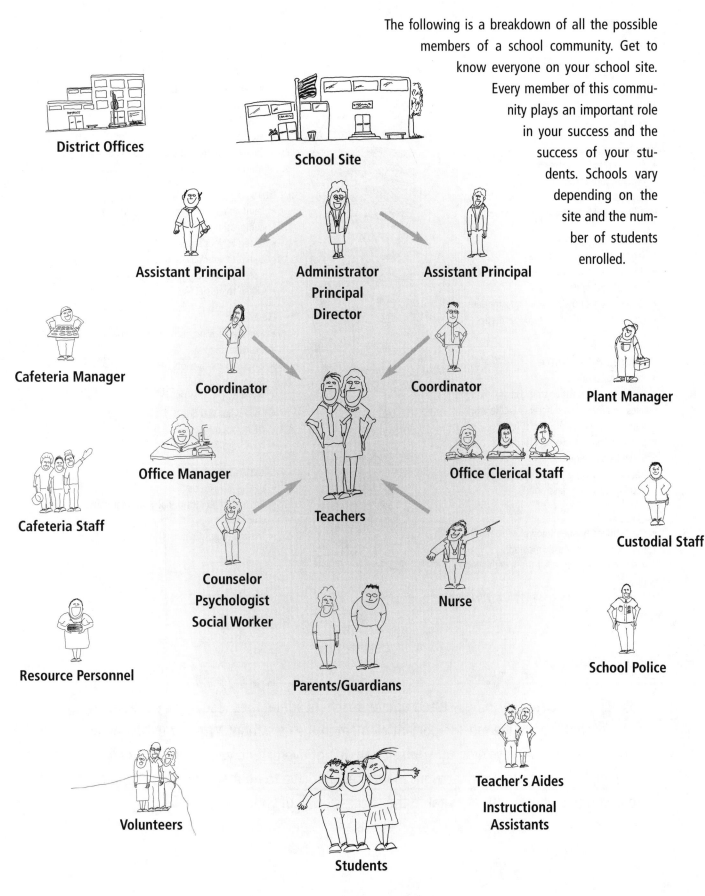

District Offices

School Site

Assistant Principal

Administrator Principal Director

Assistant Principal

Cafeteria Manager

Coordinator

Coordinator

Plant Manager

Office Manager

Office Clerical Staff

Cafeteria Staff

Teachers

Custodial Staff

Counselor Psychologist Social Worker

Nurse

Resource Personnel

Parents/Guardians

School Police

Volunteers

Students

Teacher's Aides

Instructional Assistants

Anatomy of a Teacher

Eyes
- Watch and protect your students.
- Perceive—awareness of school surroundings and the "culture" of the school.
- Observe—"read" students' faces and emotions.

Voice
- Speak up for students.
- Provide correct language usage.
- Your tone shows emotion and passion.
- Take care of your voice—try not to yell.

Hands
- Teachers are natural givers.
- Give a handshake or a pat on the back to your students every day.
- Give students positive learning experiences.
- Learn through your hands (kinesthetic learning).

Posture and Balance
- Stand up straight.
- Be proud and positive that you are changing lives and making a difference in the world you love!
- Show strength and a zest for living.
- Serve as a role model.
- Balance work and play (lots of play will keep you happy in the classroom!).

Legs
- Make things happen (movin' 'n' shakin').
- Circulate, be constantly moving.
- Provide extra support for those with special needs.
- This is the base of your strength, a good base is essential.

Brain
- Keep your mind as healthy as your body.
- Read for enjoyment.
- Know your standards.
- Keep current on educational trends and research.
- Plan great instruction.
- Take breaks from thinking; do things away from work that are fun and relaxing!

Ears
- Lend an ear and hear others out; have compassion.
- Listen to your students.
- Listen to your colleagues.
- Listen to the parents/guardians.
- Listen to music!

Heart
- Provide a loving, nurturing environment.
- Exercise daily.
- Give and receive lots of love.
- Believe in yourself.
- Believe in your students.
- Love what you do.
- Give your all.
- Love your family.

Stomach
- Eat healthy foods.
- Provide good nutritional values for your students.
- Trust your gut (instincts).

With all of the things stated above, teachers sometimes lose sight of the fact that *we* are the most important element in the classroom. Without us, learning does not go on. Always monitor yourself and do not overextend your energies. Get lots of rest, leave as much work at work as you can, and live to fight another day. Remember, you and your health are vital to the success of all of your students!

Student Overview

Students vary in personality and maturity at each grade level. The following is an overview of students at each grade level. It is important to keep in mind that this is just a general overview and that your students will vary depending on each individual.

Kindergarteners

- Can describe their needs
- Are myopic or selfish
- Have short attention spans
- Are learning to adjust to group work
- Are acquiring fine motor skills
- Need step-by-step instruction
- Are mostly familiar with personal experiences
- Enjoy singing, dancing, and pretending

First Graders

- Are not able to multitask
- Can function productively in groups
- Are conscious of others around them
- Enjoy learning through activities, games, creative stories, dancing, and singing
- Have the ability to get absorbed in tasks
- Are self-reflective in their work and seek validation
- Are most comfortable with what they already know rather than with what can actually be seen
- Have ability levels different from one another

Second Graders

- Are independent and self-sufficient but still seek validation
- Are beginning to identify details in their environment and surroundings
- Are conscious of nature and creatures
- Are risk takers, becoming confident in their abilities
- Enjoy understanding how and why things work the way they do
- Are aware of new things, such as television, the radio, movies, clothes, or toys

Third Graders

- Are enthusiastic and excited to learn new things
- Are self-reflective
- Are aware of moods
- Are aware of one another's differences
- Have a fear of not being accepted
- Are gender biased during play but cooperate in the classroom
- Test boundaries
- Are conscious of reality versus fantasy
- Are creative in writing and art

Fourth Graders

- Can distinguish seriousness versus humor
- Are aware of ability levels
- Compare work with others
- Are aware of similarities and differences
- Are conscious of popularity, music, movies, television
- Push the limits on rules
- Are specific about likes and dislikes, including subject areas
- Are responsible for their own actions
- Are introspective

Fifth Graders

- Enjoy being original in their ideas and assignments
- Take on responsibilities that might be challenging
- Are becoming problem solvers
- Work cooperatively with peers and/or in groups
- Enjoy working with their hands and producing tangible items
- Begin to be frustrated when classmates are better in subject areas such as Art, Math, sports, etc.
- Tend to be gender biased and separate based on interests
- Can work independently for longer periods of time
- Have their strengths and weaknesses—academically, athletically, and creatively—becoming more apparent

Sixth Graders

- Are sure of their knowledge and like to be right
- Are still open to new experiences
- Begin to form steadfast opinions
- Look for peer approval
- Realize that their physical changes and emotional changes cause mood swings
- Can get distracted easily at times
- Show greater interest in the media and entertainment
- Like to spend time alone, away from adults
- React positively to praised work

Seventh Graders

- Show interest in opposite sex
- Are more conscious of their physical appearance
- Are more independent and want to be treated like grown-ups
- Still show signs of childish behavior
- Are developing their identity
- Feel it is important to be accepted by peers by identifying with a group
- Are willing to engage in exciting experiences

Eighth Graders

- Are conscious about what others think of them
- Are self-conscious
- Test their roles and identities
- Have fluctuating hormones
- Are conscious of environmental responsibilities
- Wonder how their academics relate to their real-life circumstances
- Take criticism of their work personally
- Like to work with others on projects
- Are interested in abstract ideas

The
Organized
Teacher

First-Day Checklists

1

First-Day Room Checklist

☐ **Desk Arrangement** (equal access to front of room)

☐ **Teacher's Station/Desk** (where you keep all your materials/paperwork)

☐ Stapler
☐ Tape
☐ Pens, pencils
☐ Markers
☐ Notepad

☐ Referrals
☐ Supply requests
☐ Staples
☐ Paper clips
☐ Tacks

☐ **School Binder** (provided or create your own)
  ☐ Class roster, calendar
  ☐ Schedules, emergency plan, teacher/class list
  ☐ School plan/policies, discipline plan

☐ **Hall Passes** (office, nurse, boys' and girls' restroom passes)
- Make from word cards and cord.
- Label with room number (and art, if desired).
- Laminate (see template).

☐ **Welcome Sign**
- You may need a class sign to pick up class on first few days. Then attach it to the door.

☐ **Bulletin Boards**
- Blank canvasses with borders in first days
- Create them the first few weeks, then approximately every six weeks.
- Content areas: Math, Writing, Language Arts
- Social Science or Science (alternate if needed)

☐ **Calendar**
- An excellent learning tool
- Use what works for you.
- You can also purchase pocket chart version.
- Students can create or color numbers each month to match themes.

☐ **Primary Rug Station**
- Stapler, staples, scissors
- Masking and scotch tape, and tissues or paper towels
- Markers, pencils, pens, dry eraser and dry erase board, or chart paper
- Paper clips, sticky notes, and note paper
- Word cards or flash cards
- Student-lined paper and plain paper
- Extra pens, pencils, markers

☐ **Closet** (for coats and backpacks)

☐ **Centers** (Listening, Math, Writing, Science, Art)
- Introduce one at a time (one per week).
- Introduced and practiced by the whole class
- Establish center rules.
- Select independent activities.

☐ **Library**
- Group books by genre or theme.
- Place in bins or use laminated paper dividers.

☐ **Game Shelf**
- Organize games in one location.
- Introduce games one at a time (one per week).
- Establish rules and times.

☐ **Computers**
- Establish computer rules.
- Introduce to small group.
- Pair up computer buddies.

☐ **Manipulatives Shelf**
- Organize manipulatives in one location.

☐ **Table Kits**
- Crayons (in resealable bags), books, manipulatives, flash cards

☐ Board

- Teacher's name
- Aide's name
- Student count (boys, girls, total)
- Markers or chalk
- Eraser (chalk or dry)
- Dry erase spray
- Date
- Room number

☐ Classroom Rules

- The whole class establishes three to five rules.
- You guide through questioning.
- Rules should be clear, concise, comprehensive.
- Emphasize the positive (avoid "do not").

☐ Schedule

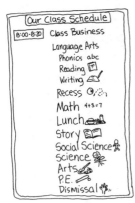

- Check for district- or state-mandated time frames (e.g., ninety minutes of P.E. per week).
- Reference other grade-level schedules.
- Use word cards/attach times = flexibility.
- Laminate.
- You may need to post daily on the board (with objectives)—check with your school.

☐ "We're Out" Sign

- Place on outside of classroom door.
- Change locations when out of room.
- Important for parents, office, and other teachers (see template)

☐ Behavior Chart

- Students collaborate on table names.
- Emphasize the positive.
- Tally points for good behavior.
- Reward winning table(s) at the end of the day.
- Note good behavior.
- Remind student(s) with incomplete work.

4

First-Day Student Checklist

Student Start-Up Items

☐ **Student Name Tags (K–1)**
(student's name, teacher's name, room number)

☐ **Desk Name Tags**
(student's first and last name)

☐ **Pencils**

K–2

2–5

☐ **Crayons**

K–1: Eight to a box

2–5: Twelve to thirty-six to a box

☐ **Paper**

Lined paper

Story paper (K–2)

Kindergarten

First

Second–third

Fourth–fifth

☐ **Student Texts or Workbooks**

☐ **Journal**
(school supplied or teacher made)

☐ **Homework Folder**

Inside   Outside

Kindergarten and first-grade folders can have:
- ABCs, numbers
- sight words
- colors
- shapes

Third- through fifth-grade folders vary (see template).

☐ **Student Information and Emergency Card**

☐ **Welcome Letter**

- Welcome/summaries
- Schedule
- Year overview
- Home study
- Attendance
- Discipline
- Curriculum

First-Day Teacher Checklist

☐ **Referral File**
- File is for all documented referrals.
- Establish a new file for each year.
- Save for three years (legal documents).

☐ **Note File**
- File is for all correspondence from home.
- Establish a new file for each year
- Note excuses on attendance record.
- Save for three years (legal documents).

☐ **Parental Consent File**
- File is for all formal consent forms. (SSTs, testing, field trips, etc.)
- Establish a new file for each year.
- Save for three years (legal documents), unless requested by office.

☐ **Referrals**
- Office and nurse referral forms
- Legal documents, save in the file marked referrals.

☐ **Role Sheet or Attendance Cards**
- Inquire about school attendance policy.
- Enter student the first day physically present.
- Record all absences.
- If excused, record and file excuse (check school policy).

☐ **Personal Information or Emergency Card**
- In office
- Check school or district policy.

☐ **Pens**
- Black is good for official documentation.

☐ **Pencils**
- No. 2 is for official forms.
- A good eraser is important!

☐ **Assorted Markers**
- Water-based for posters and cards
- Dry erase for board

☐ **Sharpie Markers**
- Permanent marker
- Excellent for illustrations
- Excellent for outlining

☐ **Overhead Markers**
- Wipes clean with water and paper towel.
- Use for overheads or laminated surface (e.g., behavior chart).

☐ **Tape**

Scotch Tape
- General taping

Masking Tape
- Heavier taping

Book-Binding Tape
- Binding and portfolios

Clear Packing Tape
- Mounting art and charts
- Portfolio binding

☐ **Sticky Putty**

☐ **Stapler and Staples**

☐ **Paper Clips**
- Both small and large are useful.

☐ **Sticky Notes**
- Very useful
- Notes, book marking, student postings, teacher's comments

☐ **Note Paper**
- Notepads are handy for writing notes to other teachers, home, etc.

☐ **Scissors**

☐ **Lined Tag**
- Tag board (lined or unlined)
- Posters, charts, portfolios (folded and bound)

☐ **Sentence Strips**
- Sentence strips
- Bulletin boards, pocket
- Charts, sequencing, labeling, etc.

☐ **Word Cards**
- Word cards (flash or word walls)
- Vocabulary, spelling, sight words, name plates, etc.

☐ **Pointer**
- Great tool for tracking and reading
- Students love to use—good reward.

☐ **Yardstick**

YARD STICK

☐ School Teacher/Room List
- Useful to have
- Contact other teachers

☐ School Procedures
- Know your school.
- Getting a sub, discipline plan
- Schedules: rain or snow, early releases
- Dismissals: regular, early
- Yard and lunch procedures

☐ Emergency Policy
- Know the protocols for your school.
- Emergency traffic patterns and exits
- Emergency kits

☐ School Policies
- Every school is different.
- Know your school and the law.
- Classroom visitors, weapons, etc.

☐ Staff Phone Tree
- Very helpful
- Subs, questions, confirmations, etc.

☐ Teacher Guidebooks
- An excellent resource
- Spend time and get to know your guides and curriculum.
- Ask other teachers how they use them.

☐ Lesson Plans
- Planning is important! Be Prepared!
- Keep up weekly—they can be part of an evaluation.
- May use objective, motivation, activity, follow-up, standard(s), evaluation (check school or district requirements)
- Tailor your plans to meet requirements, your style, and your comfort level.

☐ Grade Book
- Recording scores and assessments is important.
- It is your evidence of a student's progress.
- It is necessary for report cards, evaluations, retentions, and parent conferences.
- Get in the habit of recording each week.

Sample Room Setups

RUG

Primary Classroom Examples

Kindergarten

The kindergarten classroom is a room filled with organized activity, and it is arranged to facilitate that activity. The rug is the center of students' learning and its position is very important. Students often work in small groups facilitated by the teacher, an aide, or a parent volunteer. The flow of traffic and setup of these group stations is important for smooth transitions and minimal distractions. Establishing a routine and sticking to it will help facilitate a kindergarten classroom. Visit and observe other classrooms to see what works and why it works. Networking builds relationships and saves time! Set up your room to work for you, your students, and your program.

Do I have . . .

- sink area?
- soap, paper towels, cleanser?

Library
- Books arranged by theme

Station II
- Small-group instruction
- Materials station

Listening Center
- Books on tape
- Create your own books on tape with stories from your reading series.
- Dictate letters on tape to go with your lessons.

Station I
- Small-group instruction
- Materials station

Station III
- Small-group instruction
- Materials station

Computers

RUG

FRONT

Closet
- Storage
- Coats and backpacks

Calendar
- In the front of the room
- Resource tool

Teacher's Station
- Supplies
- Instructional materials
- Rewards

Restroom

Traffic Patterns

Components

10

First and Second Grades

The primary classroom is a place of activity. You need to consider equal access to the board and areas of instruction, traffic patterns, and your personal comfort and ease of instructional delivery. You may change the room several times throughout the year until you settle into what works for you. You may also change students' seats as you become more familiar with their personalities and work habits. Reorganization can offer a refreshing change for both you and your students.

Do I have . . .

- equal access for all students?
- a teacher's station?

Traffic Patterns

Components

Calendar
- In the front of the room
- Resource tool

FRONT

Closet
- Storage
- Coats and backpacks

Computers

- Small-group instruction
- Materials station

Library
- Books arranged by theme

RUG

- Sink area
- Soap, paper towels, and cleanser

Listening Center
- Books on tape
- Create your own books on tape with stories from your reading series and your own questions.
- Create dictations on tape to go with your lessons.

Math Station
- Numbers chart
- Chart paper
- Manipulatives

Teacher's Station
- Supplies
- Instructional materials
- Rewards

Teacher's Desk
- Teacher's filing cabinet
- Resource files
- Monthly files for holidays, events, history
- Reading and math support files
- Agendas and trainings (save for possible credential renewal hours)

First and Second Grades

This is yet another example of a first- or second-grade classroom setup. Again, you need to consider equal access to the board and areas of instruction, traffic patterns, and your personal comfort and ease of instructional delivery. In this example, the rug is in the front of the room. The rug, especially in kindergarten and first grade, is an area of primary instruction, and its location is important.

Try an arrangement for a while and see if it works for you; if it doesn't work, change it. These examples are only suggestions, and your room may be different in its setup. Using these examples and your own creativity, you can arrange your room to work for you and your students. Visit other classrooms at your grade level, too. They are an excellent resource for discovering what works.

Do I have . . .
- equal access for all students?
- a teacher's station?

Traffic Patterns

Components

Teacher's Station
- Supplies
- Instructional materials
- Rewards

Calendar
- In the front of the room
- Resource tool

Computers

Closet
- Storage
- Coats and backpacks

FRONT

RUG

- Small-group instruction
- Materials station

Library
- Books arranged by theme

- Sink area
- Soap, paper towels, and cleanser

Listening Center
- Books on tape
- Create your own books on tape with stories from your reading series and your own questions.
- Create dictations on tape to go with your lessons.

Centers
- Independent activities
- Free time or early finishers
- Set rules and rotation.

Teacher's Desk
- Teacher's filing cabinet
- Resource files
- Monthly files for holidays, events, history
- Reading and math support files
- Agendas and trainings (save for possible credential renewal hours)

Third Through Fifth Grades

Upper-grade classrooms usually do not have rugs. Instruction is done with students in their seats. It is important to have a good chair or stool when you are delivering instruction. (You will spend the majority of the time moving around the room, but a chair will offer an occasional break.) As with any grade, you need to consider equal access to the board and areas of instruction, traffic patterns, and your personal comfort and ease of instructional delivery. You may change your room as you find what works for you.

This is an example of a working classroom. Your room may be different in proportion and layout, and you may have more, less, or different furniture to arrange. This example, along with your personal creativity, can help you organize your room. It is also important to visit other classrooms to see what is working or is standard for your school. Networking is very important and saves time.

Do I have . . .

- equal access for all students?
- a teacher's station?

Teacher's Desk

- Teacher's filing cabinet
- Resource files
- Monthly files for holidays, events, history
- Reading and math support files
- Agendas and trainings

Calendar

- In the front of the room

→ **Traffic Patterns**

→ **Components**

FRONT

Closet

- Storage
- Coats and backpacks

Library

- Books arranged by theme

Computers

- Sink area
- Soap, paper towels, and cleanser

Classroom Management

Calendar

Calendars are an integral part of the classroom. They not only teach about time in days, months, and years, but they can also be a powerful tool to reinforce important math skills on a daily basis. Lower grades can use the calendar to review counting, place value, and even money. Upper grades can use it to reinforce math skills as well as learn about weather and temperature.

Remember to make your calendar work for you. Start with what you can handle then expand as you feel more comfortable. Choose a student daily or weekly to set up and lead the class in a daily calendar review.

Weather and Temperature
- You can use with past, present, and future.
- Sunny, cloudy, foggy, windy, rainy, snowy
- Hot, warm, cool, cold, freezing
- Upper grades can deal with temperature, wind speeds, barometer readings, etc.
- Weather kits can be purchased at a teacher supply store or toy store.

Postings
- Easy references and reminders
- Schedules
- School bulletins and news
- Schedule reminders

Place Value
- Ones
- Tens
- Hundreds
- Group daily.
- Move to next cup.
- Record number.
- You can record in columns.

H	T	O
	2	2

Tallies
- Record the date in tallies.
- Count by fives or ones.
- Use a heavy laminated surface and overhead markers or scrap paper.

Past, Present, Future or Days
- Practice verb tense.
- Practice days of the week.
- Expand into daily journals.
- "Write a sentence for each."
  - Today, I am . . .
  - Yesterday, I was . . .
  - Tomorrow, I will be . . .

Money Tool
- Count the date in money.
- "How many ways can we show twenty-two cents?"
  - Choose an example.
  - Show in coins.
  - Write on paper.
- Have several baggies of change.
- Use a money pocket chart.

16

Helper Chart

Assigning class jobs to students teaches responsibility, assists you in the management of your classroom, and gives students a sense of ownership over their learning environment. Students enjoy helping out and can be rotated weekly to give everyone a chance to fill each job position. One easy way to manage this is with a helper chart. This example is easy to facilitate, and you can ask other teachers how they manage this. Initially, students—especially those in the primary grades—will need to be trained to establish a routine. Find a system that works for you.

Helper Chart

office | pencil
ball | trash
door | paper
homework | line leader
nurse | jumprope
restroom | clean up

Attach with clothespins, sticky putty, etc.

Brandy A.

Kimberly B.
Michael B.
Steve S.

Students can write their own names and decorate.

A pocket chart and word cards can be used.

- Select appropriate jobs.
- Have clear expectations.
- Pair students if necessary or if they need to leave the room (office monitor).
- Students can write why they would be good for a job.
- Create a job application.

Daily Class Schedule

A class schedule needs to be posted in the classroom, giving the breakdown of your daily schedule. It should reflect a well-balanced program that includes all curricular areas. Each district or state has its own mandated minutes of instruction required for each subject area. Check with your school for a breakdown of these minutes and look at other teachers' schedules on your grade level. Adapt a schedule that meets the requirements and works for you. Some teachers leave this posted and/or write a daily schedule on the board to follow that is specific to each particular day. Schedules can change with assemblies, performances, and such, and staying flexible is important.

Do I have:

- [ ] all subject areas or activities listed?
- [ ] word cards?
- [ ] district- or state-mandated subject time blocks?
- [ ] lined tag?
- [ ] tape (clear packing)?
- [ ] sticky putty?
- [ ] markers?

- Use word cards/attach times. This gives you flexibility. You can change your schedule times as needed.

- Place time intervals on word cards and attach to the left.
- Rearrange as the schedule changes.

- Illustrate or let students illustrate.
- Cut and paste selected illustrations.

- Write the subjects on the right.

- Reference other grade-level schedules.
- Some schools may have you also post a daily schedule on board (with objectives).
- Check for district- or state-mandated time frames (e.g., ninety minutes of P.E. per week).

Door Signs

door sign is very important. Your school needs to be aware of you and your class's whereabouts in case of an emergency or if a parent/guardian needs his or her child, and a sign lets the school staff know where to find you. It is unprofessional if the school has to track you and your class down. It is easy to create a door sign that always lets others know where you are. You can use this template, and you may even choose to cut and paste it to a paper plate to create a spinner sign.

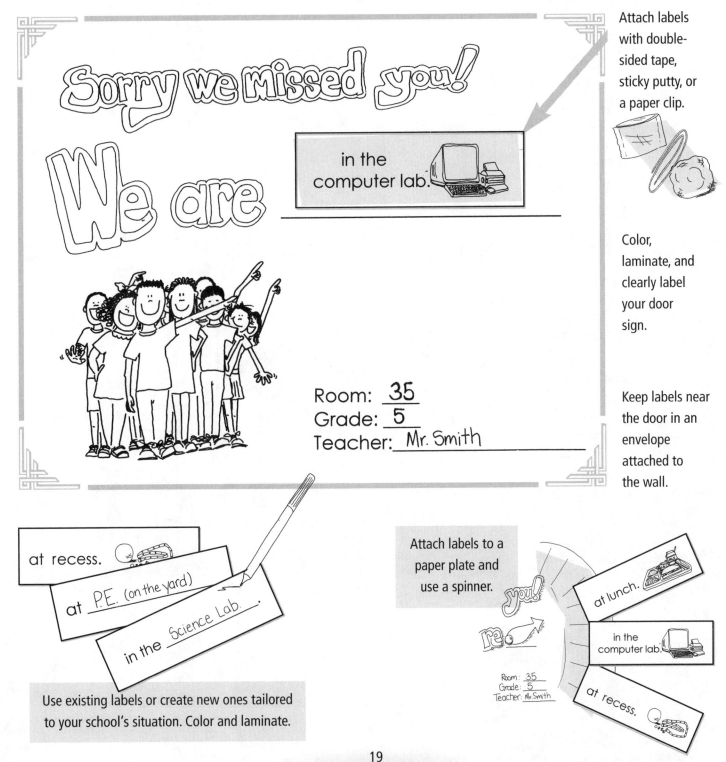

Attach labels with double-sided tape, sticky putty, or a paper clip.

Color, laminate, and clearly label your door sign.

Keep labels near the door in an envelope attached to the wall.

Sorry we missed you!

We are _____ in the computer lab.

Room: 35
Grade: 5
Teacher: Mr. Smith

at recess.
at P.E. (on the yard)
in the Science Lab.

Use existing labels or create new ones tailored to your school's situation. Color and laminate.

Attach labels to a paper plate and use a spinner.

you! re

at lunch.
in the computer lab.
at recess.

Room: 35
Grade: 5
Teacher: Mr.Smith

Sorry we missed you!

We are

Room: _____ Grade: _____

Teacher: _____

Door Sign

Color and cut out sign and location tags. Laminate.

Post sign on door so administrators, parents, and other teachers will know where you are when not in the classroom.

Keep tags in an envelope mounted on inside wall of classroom.

Use putty or tape to attach the tag denoting your class location when not in the room.

This is a great job for a monitor! Even younger students can read labels with visual clues.

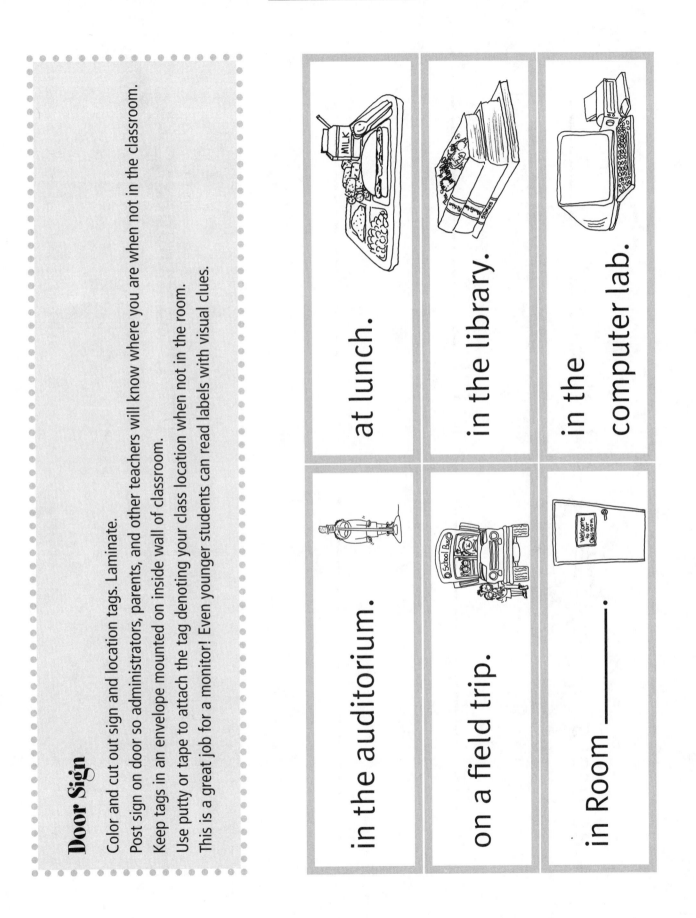

at lunch.

in the library.

in the computer lab.

in the auditorium.

on a field trip.

in Room _____.

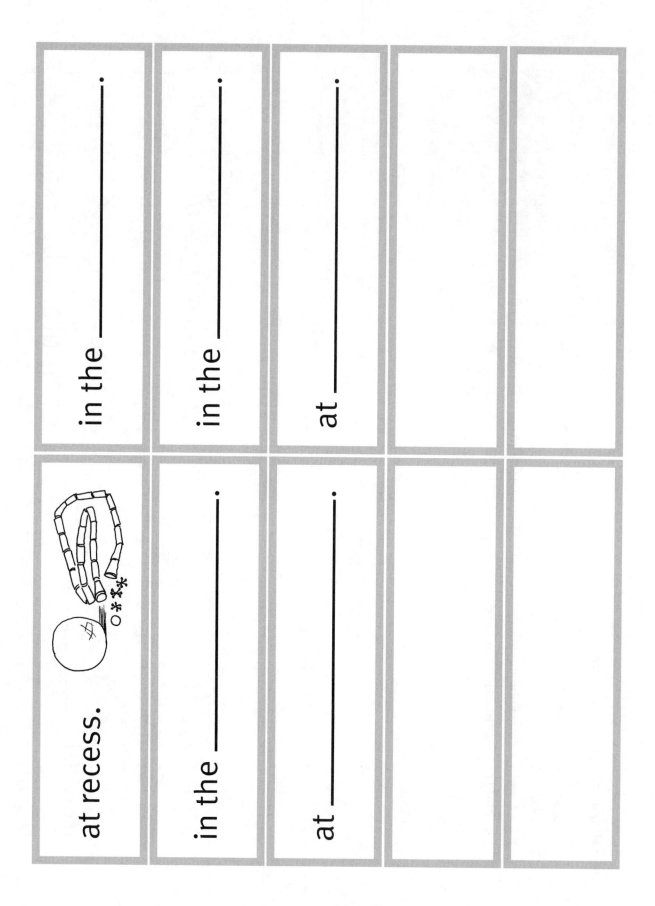

in the _____.

in the _____.

at _____.

at recess.

in the _____.

at _____.

Boy Pass

Teacher: _____

Grade: _____

Room: _____

Girl Pass

Teacher: _____

Grade: _____

Room: _____

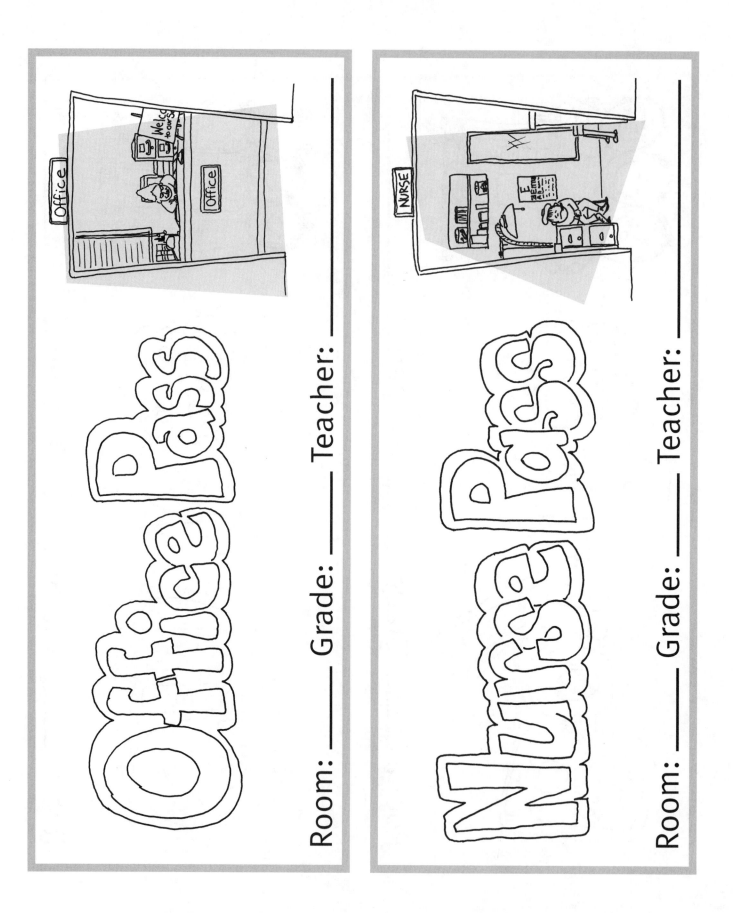

Office Pass

Room: _____ Grade: _____ Teacher: _____

Nurse Pass

Room: _____ Grade: _____ Teacher: _____

School Binder

Having school information and policies at your quick disposal can be very important in facilitating an organized classroom. Many schools provide you with a binder containing their policies and procedures. Some schools provide you with bulletins that contain this information. You will refer to them throughout the year, and establishing and maintaining a binder is an excellent way to manage this paperwork. Create one that works for you. Always update it with any new material you receive. These are suggestions for what to include.

Teacher/Room List
- Useful to have
- Can contact other teachers

School Procedures
- Know your school.
- Getting a sub
- Discipline plan
- Schedules: rain or snow early releases
- Dismissals: regular, early
- Yard and lunch procedures

Emergency Policy
- Know protocols for your school.
- Know emergency traffic patterns and exits.
- Emergency kits

School Information
- Very helpful for grant writing
- School population and make-up
- Services
- Resources

Staff Phone Tree
- Very helpful
- Subs, questions, confirmations, etc.

School Policies
- Every school is different.
- Know your school and the law.
- Classroom visitors
- Retention
- Releasing a student
- Attendance and absences
- Support referrals and testing

Schedules
- Daily school hours
- Current school calendar
- Holidays
- Vacations
- Minimum, shortened days
- Teacher work days
- Conferences
- Reporting periods
- Duty schedule

Classroom Information
- Class roster
- Student phone list
- Special or pull-out student programs
- Reporting grade sheets

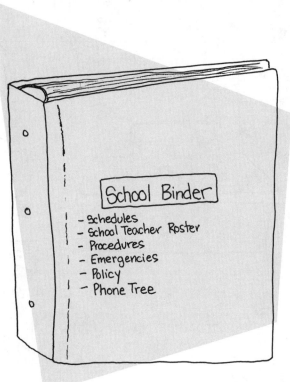

School Binder
- Schedules
- School Teacher Roster
- Procedures
- Emergencies
- Policy
- Phone Tree

- Three-ring binder (about a two-inch one)
- Plastic sheet protectors

Student Table Kits

Student table kits are a great way to organize student materials. Some teachers use bins, baskets, or small containers. Use what you are most comfortable with and what works best with your students. Visit other rooms to see how other teachers manage student materials, books, etc. Tabletop bins are helpful because they can hold a variety of materials, and students can even share bins. Having students maintain their materials can be incorporated into the table point reward system—it is an excellent opportunity to teach responsibility and sharing.

Markers or Color Pencils (if available)
or
Pencils (grade appropriate)

Books
- Readers
- Theme related
- Stories read in class

Resource Cards
- Sight words
- Unit vocabulary
- Prefixes and suffixes card
- Times table

Flash Cards

Manipulatives Bag*
- Money
- Unifix cubes
- Tens/ones sticks (label with tape)

Crayons (grade appropriate)
- Table caddies also make an excellent way to manage your crayons.

Glue Stick or Glue
- Know your students; add to bin only if they can handle it.

---

*Create your own manipulatives (e.g., tens/ones sticks with popsicle sticks and beans). Buttons and macaroni can be used as counters. Macaroni can be dyed different colors using rubbing alcohol and food coloring. Place alcohol, food coloring, and macaroni in a resealable bag. Once desired color shade is reached, empty the bag and dry the pasta.

Classroom Rules and Behavior Management

Classroom Rules

Classroom rules are a necessity. Keeping them clear, concise, and comprehensive is important. As a great first-day activity, students can collectively establish their classroom rules, which will give them ownership of their classroom. This in turn creates an understanding of what is expected and clear expectations. Students are more likely to follow what they have established than what they are told. You, as the teacher, can guide your students to establish a set of fundamental rules that work for you and them. Three is a good number of rules for the lower grades and five for the upper grades. Keep in mind that they need to be specific. State the rule with positive wording—emphasize the "Do's" and avoid the "Don'ts."

Too Specific

OUR CLASSROOM RULES
1. Raise your hand when you have a question.
2. Don't hit.
3. Listen to the teacher.

Better

OUR CLASSROOM RULES
1. Raise your hand.
2. Keep your hands and feet to yourself.
3. Listen when others speak.

Creating Your Classroom Rules

1. Discuss rules. Ask your students, "Why do we need rules?" "What rules should we have in our classroom?"
2. Take suggestions from the whole class in group discussion and record on the board.
3. Challenge proposed rules: "If that is a rule, what happens if . . . ?" "How could we say that differently?"
4. Vote on three rules that everyone agrees on (five for upper grades).
5. Write the rules on half a sheet of tag poster board in manuscript or cursive.
6. Add a drawing to make it more appealing. Students can color and even do the drawing.
7. Laminating it will help it hold up better.
8. Review with class and display in the front of the room where all can see.

Activities

Students can record rules and illustrate them to take home and share with their parents.

Students can create consequences for not following the rules.

Students can write stories about a student who doesn't follow the rules.

Classroom Behavior

It always helps to use some type of behavior system in your classroom. Students like structure! This behavior system can be designed specifically for your classroom. The different methods used to promote excellent behavior will make your job easier. The type of behavior method—how it works and the rules that are applied—can be left up to your imagination. These are some ideas to help you get started or to give you fresh ideas.

- Let the students control the chart, the more in charge the children are, the more powerful this tool will be for you.

- Share your behavior plan with students' parents so they know what to expect from your class and what they should expect of their child.

- Make your behavior program as positive as possible—intrinsic rewards should always be the goal—even if the reward is good grades, a note home, or free time on the computer.

- Be consistent. Whatever your program may be, consistency works best!

- Keep your reward or behavior system or chart in an open, visible place. Having students see it will help reinforce the message.

- Evaluate your behavior modification program frequently and make changes if necessary.

- *Upper grades* (6–12)—Other behavior methods can be used that are more appropriate for the age of students you are teaching. For upper grades, try charts or graphs for no tardies, completed assignments, and homework finished.

- Make this system work for you! If your method is too difficult, too time consuming, or not working, try something new. What has worked for one year may not work for the next. Change is good!

Classroom Behavior Ideas

These ideas may help you set up a system for managing student behavior within your classroom. Remember to try new things, make modifications, and see what works best for you. Students respond best to positive feedback and praise!

1. Behavior Chart

This is a chart where every student has a pocket with color-coded cards that are pulled as warnings. Each color has its own consequence or reward.

2. Name Cards

You can make cards for all of your students and give out stickers or stamps if they perform well or have good behavior. You can create a reward per number of stars earned.

3. Names on Chalkboard

Create a chart or list on the chalkboard where names can be written. For every good action, the student receives a check mark. This should only be used as a positive reward type of list.

4. Individual Behavior Cards

These cards can be used for individual students as you see fit. Again, these can have a student's name with a place to receive a star or a smiley face for good behavior.

Classroom Behavior Management Chart

Behavior management is vital to your success and the success of your students. Consistency is the key. Teams (four to six students) work well to teach cooperation and accountability. It is important to mix the students so that the teams are fair. Occasionally, a student has difficulty with the team effort; when this happens, see the progress and growth that has been made and award points based on that. If a student continues to affect the team, discuss the situation with the student and the team. If it continues, that student is making a choice not to reap the rewards of the team.

Do I have:

☐ Fair teams (mixed behavior levels)?
☐ Tables assigned to teams?
☐ Team-selected names?
☐ Understanding of rewards and consequences?

Table Points

Lions — ⊞⊞ ‖ — 7 — Table 1
Bears — ⊞ — 5 — Table 2
Tigers — ⊞ ‖ — 6 — Table 3
Sharks — ⊞ ‖‖ — 8 — Table 4
Eagles — ‖‖ — 3 — Table 5

☆ Behavior ☆ Stars ☆ — Needs to Complete
Mary Juan — Pedro - home study
Sam — Jan - seat work

- Teams can collaboratively select their own name and sit at the same table(s).

- Tallies are given throughout the day. The teacher is ultimately in control and can "catch" a table doing well, hence can make it work to their advantage.

- Laminate and use overhead markers or mount team names to board and use chalk.

- Winning table(s) receive(s) reward (extra play, candy, early release to lunch or recess, etc.). Depending on needs, this can be at recess, at lunch, or at the end of the day (wean to longer stretches of time).

- Can post names of students who need to complete assignment.
  - No recess
  - No free time

- Reserved for excellent behavior

Note poor behavior.

Warning system:
1. Name on teacher clipboard ✓
2. Time out (five minutes) ✓✓
3. Office referral ✓✓✓
4. Note home ✓✓✓✓

Erase letter by letter as behavior improves

Classroom Incentives

Classroom incentives give students goals to achieve. These can serve as a motivation for the entire class or individual students. For incentive goals to work, you need to provide clear expectations and follow through on them. Incentive goals encourage teamwork and cooperation within the class. Individually, these goals can keep a student focused on a behavior or an academic goal. It is important to make each goal realistic and obtainable. Younger students will need a shorter wait time or reward/consequence time than older students. It is important to know your students and when they need to be encouraged or possibly rewarded. Be flexible, and allow them to know success. They can be weaned into longer intervals once a pattern is established.

Desired behavior goals can range from paying attention and participating during a lesson to staying on task and completing assignments. Desired academic goals can range from applying a grammar skill appropriately to achieving individual reading goals. Keep in mind that academic achievements will vary, so individual achievement must always be considered first, and then collective growth across all levels can be rewarded.

Whole-Class Incentives

Fill the Jar

- Students collectively fill a jar with marbles, jellybeans, etc.
- Each time students demonstrate desired behavior as a collective group or in small groups, a marble or selected object is added to the jar, and the jar is slowly filled.
- Once the jar is filled, the class is rewarded with a designated prize.

Note: Keep the goal obtainable. Start with a smaller jar to establish a pattern.

Stars

- Set up a chart to record a designated number of stars.
- Class receives stars for desired behavior.
- Once star count reaches the established number, a reward is given.

Note: Keep number obtainable; start with a lower number and then increase.

Fill the Fish Tank

- A fish tank, if permissible in your district, can be set up with no fish.
- Students can earn points to use toward adding fish to the tank.

Note: Always check district policy regarding animals in the classroom.

Fish Bowl

- Students can keep fish bowl or class pet at their table for the day.
- Students can earn points to use toward keeping the pet for a day.

Note: Always check district policy regarding animals in the classroom.

Table Points

- Table teams are established and given names.
- Tally points are given for desired table behaviors throughout the day.
- Winning tables are rewarded daily at dismissal.
- Rewards can include stickers, pencils, snacks, etc.

Note: Table groups can be renamed according to themes (animals, modes of transportation, etc.).

Cushion Reward

- Students whose table group collectively wins the most points or achieves a set goal win the use of seat cushions for the week.

Note: Use the cushions that tie on to avoid slipping.

Individual Student Incentives

Popcorn Party

- Plan a popcorn or snack party prior to dismissal on Fridays
- Students who have received points for good behavior (an established number, e.g., three checks) can participate.
- This is very powerful.

Note: If permissible in your district, you can use a hot air popper, as the smell adds to the excitement. Always check first.

Sticker or Stamp Cards

- Index cards can be taped to each student's desk.
- Stickers or stamps are given for desired behavior.
- A set number is rewarded.
- Good for homework, class work, participation, etc.

Individual Student Contract

- This is a personalized contract of behavior modifications. Teacher and student establish contract. Each student's input is important and helpful on his or her own contract (establishes meaning and purpose).
- Goals are explicit and concise.
- Student is observed throughout day and checked off on behavior.
- The contract is sent home daily or weekly for the parent/guardian to sign.

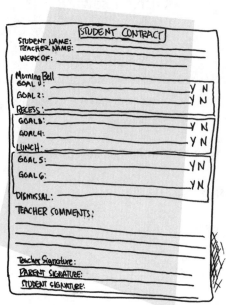

Citizen of the Week

- Students who have a good week (demonstrate good school citizenship) receive a weekly Good Citizenship Award.
- Can be as simple as an index card with a sticker labeled "Good Citizen."
- Establish clear expectations, as with any reward.
- Notify parents to expect this weekly reward.
- Students are warned with name on board and further with checks beside name.
- Establish a set number of checks that would prevent students from getting their award and how they can work to remove checks and name.

Tickets

- Students earn tickets throughout the day.
- Students visit a prize chest on Fridays and exchange tickets for prizes.
- Prizes have established values.

  Note: To avoid conflicts, always have students put their name on their tickets and keep in a resealable bag with their name on it.

Student Checkbooks

- Students earn "money" for good behavior throughout the day or week.
- Students deposit and balance their checkbooks.
- Students use "money" to write checks for prizes.
- Prizes have designated values.

Behavior Contracts

These behavior contracts are to help you with particular students who have a hard time following rules. Of course, you can always make your own behavior contracts that pertain directly to the student you are working with. These contracts are helpful when you are dealing with a student who just can't stay on task, is unable to raise his or her hand, or does not complete in-class assignments. These contracts, when used with several positive rewards, can help you to get the desired behavior you want out of that student. These can definitely modify a student's learning and provide one more layer of structure for them to be successful within the classroom. Hopefully, these contracts will make your job of educating these particular types of students better. Good luck!

- Circle the face depending on the student's performance on the particular goal.
- This behavior contract is more for daily behavior modification. Choose three specific desired behaviors.
- Send this card home each day to have the parent/guardian sign it.

Student's Name __Victor Burnett__   Date __7/8/05__

Three goals this student will be working on...

1 Staying in his seat during work time.

2 Raising his hand before talking.

3 Keeping his hands to himself. ✗ super

Parent Signature __Tina Burnett__

- This contract is a weekly behavior contract. The card can be sent home at the end of the five days.
- Each time the student demonstrates the desired behavior, a positive mark is given (try using star stickers, stamps, or a Bingo inker).
- Both contracts work well with the student receiving some type of reward for getting all positives or mostly positives.

Name __Brandt Christopher__   Daily Behavior for the week of __August 9th__
Parent signature __Carly Christopher__

	Early Morning	Late Morning	After Lunch	Late Afternoon	Dismissal
Monday	☆	☆	—	☆	☆
Tuesday	☆	☆	☆	☆	☆
Wednesday	☆	☆			
Thursday					
Friday					

Student's Name: _____ Date: _____

Three goals this student will be working on:

1. _____

2. _____

3. _____

Parent's Signature: _____

Name: _____ Daily Behavior for the Week of: _____

	Early Morning	Late Morning	After Lunch	Late Afternoon	Dismissal
Monday					
Tuesday					
Wednesday					
Thursday					
Friday					

Parent's Signature: _____

WEEKLY ATTENDANCE AWARD

This award certifies that

_____

has perfect attendance for the week of

_____.

Mr./Mrs./Ms. _____ Principal: _____

Weekly Attendance Award

This award certifies that

_____

has perfect attendance for the week of

_____.

Mr./Mrs./Ms. _____ Principal: _____

Certificate of

ACHIEVEMENT

presented to

for perfect attendance for the month of

Principal

Teacher

Certificate of

ACHIEVEMENT

presented to

_____

for perfect attendance for the month of

_____ .

_____
Teacher

_____
Principal

CERTIFICATE OF
ACHIEVEMENT

PRESENTED TO

PERFECT ATTENDANCE FOR THE YEAR!

YEAR

PRINCIPAL

TEACHER

Certificate of

ACHIEVEMENT

Presented to

Perfect Attendance for the Year!

_____
YEAR

_____
Teacher

_____
Principal

Classroom Organization

Parent Letter

Communication home is very important. A good opening letter to parents/guardians can set the tone for the year and accomplish a great deal. Never send a letter home, however, unless it has been approved by the school. Check with your school for its policy regarding sending letters home. Also ask other teachers what they send home.

Create a letter that is personal and outlines your goals and policies. Here are some tips and ideas about what you may want to include in your letter home.

Policies and Procedures:
- Daily agenda
- Home-study policy and expectations
- Classroom rules
- Attendance policy
- School calendar
- Emergency contact form
- Sign and return portion
- Field-trip procedure
- Suggested materials needed

Home Support Suggestions:
- Read twenty minutes a day.
- Ask questions about what students read.
- Practice counting (primary).
- Practice multiplication facts.
- Practice spelling words orally.
- Go to the library.

Teacher:
- Be positive!
- Be concise and to the point.
- Tell a little bit about yourself.
- Give school contact information for your contact info.

School Information (check for):
- School contract or rules
- School calendar
- Testing calendar
- Emergency cards
- Lunch forms
- Student release forms

Goals and Expectations:
- Standards covered at grade level
- Goals you have established
- Behavior expectations
- Home support expectations

Classroom Organization

Organizing your classroom can keep it running smoothly throughout the day. Training your students in organizational procedures is important, and the first few weeks of school are critical in laying the foundations for your classroom. Organizing class work in a specific location makes for easy access. Having a designated home-study basket helps with its distribution. An office basket by the door is a convenient drop-off for anything from the office and limits interruptions. A designated home-study folder box keeps folders organized and makes for easy preparation when going home. A work template file box allows you to organize and file extras of your favorite resource templates and access them easily.

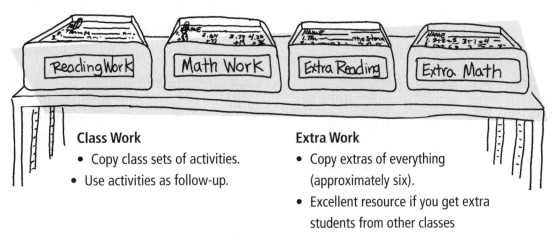

Class Work

- Copy class sets of activities.
- Use activities as follow-up.

Extra Work

- Copy extras of everything (approximately six).
- Excellent resource if you get extra students from other classes
- Provides work for early finishers

Home-Study Basket

- Holds daily home study
- Easy to distribute

Office Basket

- Paperwork from office
- Easy to access or distribute
- Keep near door.

Work Templates

- Organize resource templates.
- Copy extras so they are always available.
- Story papers, spelling forms, writing templates, etc.

Home-Study Folders

- Classroom monitor collects daily.
- Classroom monitor fills with new work each day.
- Easy access if student leaves early

Writing Table

Organizing your writing table can make the writing process easier to facilitate. Having extra templates for each stage really helps. Consistency and repetition are the keys to successful writing. It is helpful to designate one location where students' ongoing writing folders and writing portfolios (completed work) are easily accessible. Making overheads of your writing templates or paper can be helpful to model writing and whole-class writing. They are also helpful in singling out a particular skill (e.g., write a piece void of adjectives or capitals and then have the class model the editing on the overhead). It is best to focus on one skill and then apply it to students' writing.

Writing Process Templates

Writing-in-Progress Folders

Writing Portfolios

Writing Table

Plain Paper

Lined Paper

Possible Writing Templates or Paper

- Story starters (first sentence given, students complete)
- Letter template
- Theme paper (theme-related shape or border, e.g., bunny shape)
- Story paper (lines and illustration space)
- Minibook template pages
- Book-report forms

Portfolios

Student portfolios are a place for students to keep their best work. As with any portfolio, they should be reviewed periodically to update the work. Students can add or dictate why they have chosen a particular work. A handful of work (up to ten pieces) can be kept in the portfolio. Portfolios can be used at parent conferences, with students sharing their best work and reflections. You may have separate folders for work samples that you choose to keep (work folders). Students can be easily trained to maintain their own portfolios. Younger students may need to be reminded or asked, "Do you want to put this in your portfolio?" It is easy to add items and then periodically review the portfolios as a whole, selecting approximately the best ten items to stay.

Front

- Tag (full or half sheet)
- Folded and taped
- (Large size is great for art assignments that are selected.)

Back

- Leave room for name.

- Students can draw quarterly self-portraits to show growth.

- Book-binding tape or clear packing tape

Work Folder
- Your selections
- Evidence of work progress

Assessment and writing portfolios can also be maintained. Check with your school's requirements for record keeping. Writing portfolios house students' writing assignments throughout the year. Assessment portfolios hold all formal assessments given throughout the year. Both have cover pages (found in the "Portfolios" section of this book) that attach to the outside of the folder and can be used to record results.

Assessment Boxes

Assessment boxes are an important tool for teaching. These boxes, composed of students' work, can provide you with important feedback on a student's progress within your class. These various boxes can also be useful during parent conferences or meetings with an administrator. Although you may currently have a system in place, these are just a few ideas as to how you could add to your already successful program or simply begin a few of these boxes.

For a colorful box, try going to a local office supply store and get colored folders.

Folders are easy to locate with good labels. Try creating a sheet that goes on the front of each folder that tells the contents of that particular folder. Some folder covers are included in this book (see "Portfolios") if you do not want to make your own.

Your students' portfolios can contribute to your grading as well as to filling out report cards.

There should be a current folder for each student in each box.

Three assessment boxes we recommend are Writing, Math, and Assessments.

Your portfolio boxes should be in a visible place in your room so that anyone walking in can see where they are. Easy access to these is always a good idea!

Easy-to-read labels can save you a lot of time when you are trying to locate a particular box or a student's folder.

Filing Cabinet Ideas

Filing cabinets can be a great source for organization within any classroom. Teachers often become inundated with thousands of papers, assessments, notes, and some super worksheets! Using files can save you the headache of a messy room, lost thematic units, and fogginess in your own mind. Below are a few different types of files you may wish to keep or add to your already exceptional file system. Remember that these are to just get you started—try thinking of other titles you can use as a folder.

Holidays

- Halloween
- Thanksgiving
- Christmas
- Valentine's Day
- St. Patrick's Day
- Easter
- Fourth of July

Class Subjects

- Math
- Science
- Art
- Language Arts
- Social Studies
- Physical Education
- Literature
- Health/Nutrition

Themes

- Pirates
- Plants
- Dinosaurs
- Ancient Egypt
- Solar System
- Sea life
- Birds
- Animals
- Native American civilizations
- Continents
- Family
- Games
- Homes
- Life cycles
- Transportation
- The market
- Community helpers
- Farms

Types of Writing

- Poetry
- Short stories
- Letters
- Descriptive
- Recipes
- Informative
- Procedures

Months

- September
- October
- November
- December
- January
- February
- March
- April
- May
- June
- July
- August

Movement Within the Classroom

No matter what grade level or subject you teach, you can establish some patterns and rules for how students move throughout the classroom. Traffic patterns can be very open-ended and probably pertain more to the elementary setting. If you do use traffic patterns in your classroom, remember to give lots of reminders and practice with the students. A great way to create these patterns is as a class, which helps students "buy in" more easily. Once you begin to have students move in the correct direction, stick to it! These patterns can also be used if you're teaching sixth through twelfth grades or such classes as Art or Science Lab, which have equipment that requires caution.

Remember to:

- keep these patterns simple!
- establish a rhythm.
- streamline transitions.
- review daily.

Reasons for Use:

- Getting and putting away backpacks
- Lining up for recess and dismissal
- Going to and from the rug
- Emergencies

Try:

- different patterns.
- asking other teachers for advice and about what they do to succeed.
- using a signal to get students moving in the right direction.

Classroom Centers

Classroom Centers

Classroom centers are an important part of self-learning and exploration. They can range from an organized station on a desktop to a designated area in the room for an activity. A rotation can be established so that students move from center to center and everyone gets a turn. Centers do not have to be complex or involved. Set up centers that support your themes or units. Earlier finishers can go to their favorite center, but watch out for students who rush to get through early just to go to centers. Training your students that early finishers must still present quality work before they can move on to centers is important. Liken their work to their "ticket" to a center. Establish an order: first, assigned seat work (tasks 1, 2, and 3); second, a choice from the extra work basket; third, a center. Have students check each other's work for quality and accuracy, sign each other off, then proceed to centers. It is nice to have enough thought-out center activities, from established centers to a simple game, so that your entire class can participate if need be.

Always introduce a center to the class and establish center rules. Students can work in pairs.

Center Ideas

Math Center

Ten Activity Ideas
1. Counting or sorting
2. Weighing (scale)
3. Measuring (ruler), e.g., string
4. Story problems
5. Flash cards
6. Tangrams (geometric patterns)
7. Practicing fact sheets or timers
8. Calculators
9. Measurement in volumes
10. Problem of the day

Science Center

Ten Activity Ideas
1. Growing beans in baggies
2. Magnifying glass (observations)
3. Electricity (battery or lightbulb)
4. Magnets (metal vs. nonmetal)
5. Animal or dinosaur models
6. Simple machines
7. Life cycle (butterflies, tadpoles)
8. Sink or float
9. Reactions (simple)
10. Classroom pet (approved)

Note: General activity is observing, recording observations, and illustrating.

Publishing Center

Ten Activity Ideas

1. Writing about a magazine or calendar picture
2. Creating a minibook
3. Creating a comic strip
4. Finishing a story starter
5. Creating a bound book
6. Writing a poem
7. Writing a letter (to a friend or a character)
8. Creating a greeting card
9. Writing a story on a theme template
10. Writing directions or instructions to a prompt

Note: Desks make great centers and provide extra storage. Students can keep ongoing activities in a folder.

Clay Table

Clay Table Hints

- Cover desk with tag and tape down edges.
- Do not place the desk in the sun.
- Clay colors will mix together.
- Students need to wash hands—clay can be messy.
- Excellent for increased dexterity.
- Students of all ages love it!

Rug Center (Primary)

Ten Activity Ideas

1. Board games
2. Building sets
3. Puzzles
4. Teacher's station (playing school)
5. Dress-up (trunk)
6. Animal figures
7. Train set
8. Doll house
9. Electronic games (portable)
10. Marbles or jacks

Note: Can have up to about six at the rug

Listening Center

Listening Center Hints

- Train students to use a cassette or CD player.
- Use books on tape or create your own.
- Activities can be interactive, e.g., dictation, questions.
- Store books and their tapes in resealable bags.
- Number or color code books and tapes.
- Just tape ideas you can create:
  - Reread a chapter (any subject).
  - Dictate math problems.
  - Dictate spelling or vocabulary.
  - Ask review questions, and have students write response.
- Have pencils and paper at the station.

Computer Center

Computer Hints

- Always introduce each game to the class.
- Find a dependable student who is good with computers and train him or her to assist.
- Have a computer sign-in to keep track of visits.
- Have a set of established rules.

Sample Rules

1. Play only the currently set game.
2. Take turns.
3. Only print with permission.
4. Use the computer with care and respect.
5. Leave the computer as you found it.

Tracking Your Students' Computer Time

Tracking Hints

- Establish an order.
- Students can sign in and date their turn.
- Rotate through the whole class.
- A clothespin list is another excellent option.
- Have a student monitor maintain rotation.
- When finished, each student can notify the next student on the list to continue the rotation.

Each time a student is finished, he or she removes the clothespin, places it in cup, and calls the next student (skipping any absent students).

Painting Center

Painting Center Hints

- Cover floor area under easel with butcher paper or plastic and secure with tape.
- Have a smock or large shirt available for painters to wear.
- Use paint containers with lids to avoid drying out paints.
- Establish procedures, especially clean-up.
- Schools usually provide classes with easels.

Art Center

Art Center Hints

- Always introduce and work with a medium several times prior to placing in the art center.
- Establish rules for the center and for each medium's use.
- Save paper scraps for the center. (A good rule: We save the scrap if it is larger than our hand.)
- Paper towels, wet wipes, etc., should be handy.
- Allow students to explore and create freely.
- A sign-in is a good idea—this is a popular center! Use a clipboard or a chipboard and a clamp to create a sign-in.
- Desks make the best art centers. You can utilize the insides for storage.

Classroom Library

Classroom libraries are an integral part of every classroom. A classroom library is an excellent way to organize your books. This allows for easy access to theme-based collections of books. Students, too, can easily find books related to themes that they are interested in. As your collection of books grows, you can keep them organized by using plastic bins or even laminated colored paper markers. Clearly label both for easy access. Choose an organization that aligns with the themes and subjects you are teaching within your grade level. Again, set it up to work for you. Visit other classrooms to see how they have organized their libraries and how they manage their books.

Science
- Animals
- Plants
- Fish
- Insects
- Physical Science
- Earth Science
- Weather

Social Science
- Community
- Historical figures
- History
- Multicultural
- Wars
- Regions
- Presidents
- Civics

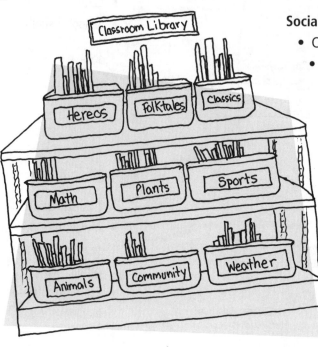

Literature
- Folktales and fairy tales
- Poetry
- Informative
- Historical
- Trade books
- Core literature chapter books

Other
- Holidays
- Sports
- Crafts
- Art

Stories
- Characters
- Multicultural
- Language
- Ethnicity
- Religion
- Gender related
- Immigration and migration
- Family
- Friendship
- People with disabilities

Math
- Place books with math-related topics together.

Helpful Tips:

- Start with general themes, and, as the library grows, subdivide them (e.g., animals into mammals, reptiles, amphibians, and fish).
- Mark, number, or color-code the books for easy management.
- Organize books by ability level.
- Create a library area, a comfortable place to read (e.g., a rug, pillows, a table and chairs, etc.).

Classroom Tools

School Supplies

Schools often provide supplies. You may have to request them from a designated secretary or your school supply room. Your designated supply person is a very important friend! Anticipate holiday and project needs early to assure proper supplies. Each school is different. Some schools have some or all supplies (e.g., student writing paper) available in an open room. Ask your office staff how this is handled.

- Supply request forms are usually in a designated location—an office or supply room.

- They may have a carbon copy.

- Supplies may be picked up or delivered depending on school policy.

Color Ordering Considerations
(These colors are popular and need to be requested early!)

September, October, November (fall, Halloween, Thanksgiving)
- Orange, yellow, brown, black, white, purple

December, January (Christmas, Hanukah, Kwanza, winter)
- Red, green, white, blue, orange, yellow

February (Valentine's Day, African-American History Month, Presidents' Day)
- Pink, red, white, green, yellow, black

March, April, May, June (Saint Patrick's Day, Easter, spring)
- Green, yellow, white, pink

July, August (Fourth of July, summer)
- Red, white, blue

Paper

Copy Paper	Ream of Paper	Small Construction Paper (9 × 12″)	Large Construction Paper (12 × 18″)	Graph Paper (Math— upper grades)

Lined Paper

Kindergarten
10½" 8" 1⅛"

First
10½" 8" ⅝"

Second–third
10½" 8" ½"

Fourth–fifth
8½" 11"

Story Paper

Journals
My Journal
-Pam Smith
Room 4

Word Cards or Sentence Strips
(flash cards, vocabulary, name plates, hall passes)

Tag or Poster Board
(lined or unlined)
(charting, posters)

Chipboard
(good for testing dividers)

Index Cards
(notes, name tags, student input)

Arts and Crafts

Yarn

Cord (heavy yarn)

Brads (fasteners)

Glue
GLUE

Rubber Cement
RUBBER CEM

Glue Stick
GLUE STICK

59

Student Scissors

Glue Bottles

Tempera Paint

Watercolor Paint

Paint Container
(fill with liquid paint)

Tissue Paper

Round Paintbrush

Flat Paintbrush

Felt

Pipe Cleaners

Rings (large/medium/small)

Clothespins

Liquid Starch

Clamps or Clips

Markers

Primary Crayons (K–2)

Standard Crayons (2–5)

CRAYON

MARKERS

Primary Pencils (K–2)

Pencils (2–5)

Teacher

Chalk
(yellow or white) (colored)

Eraser

Dry Erase Markers

Scotch Tape (individual or dispenser)

Masking Tape (thick and thin)

Clear Packing Tape (mounting, binding)

Book-Binding Tape (book repairs, portfolio edges)

File Folders

Stapler

Staples

Staple Remover

Markers

Water Based Marker

Overhead Markers

OVERHEAD MARKER

Pens

Pencils

Permanent Markers

PERMANENT MARKER.

Paper Clips

Sticky Notes

Butcher Paper (assorted colors)

Sticky Putty

STICKY

Scissors

Teacher's Workstation

Teacher's workstations are basically all your materials organized in one location, making them easily accessible. When strategically located, workstations can save you time and help things run smoothly. Personalize your workstation with items you use in your instruction and facilitation of the classroom. Office supply stores sell inexpensive storage units that you can use, or you can create your own system. Having these materials at your fingertips avoids interruptions while someone searches for the stapler or scissors. You can house instructional materials here as well. Flash cards, learning games, minibooks—whatever you may be using at the time and need readily accessible. Again, make this a system that works for you and select supplies that you use. Being organized is the key to a well-run classroom. Visit other classrooms and see how other teachers organize their materials.

Materials:

☐ Pens
☐ Pencils
☐ Markers
☐ Sticky notes
☐ Eraser
☐ Stapler
☐ Staples
☐ Scissors
☐ Tape
☐ Masking tape
☐ Glue stick
☐ Paper clips
☐ Word cards
☐ Paper

Resources:

☐ Flash cards
☐ Decodables or readers
☐ Learning games

Teacher's Math Workstation

Math workstations are a helpful way to organize your math instructional materials and manipulatives. If you are teaching a primary grade, you may find it helpful to set up an easel, using the tray to hold your things and the easel as a writing or poster surface. If you are teaching an upper grade, you can organize these items in an area that is easily accessible and near the front of the room or focal point of instruction.

The idea is that you are not scrambling for materials so that your instructional delivery is as smooth as possible. When teachable moments arise throughout the day, you are ready. Visit other teachers and see what manipulatives they use for their math instruction.

Chart Paper
- Math problems
- Class-generated story problems
- Counting
- Number play
- Etc.

Number Chart
- Counting
- More and less
- $\pm$

Flash Cards
(purchased or created)
- Math facts

Money Manipulatives
- Counting money
- $\pm$ Money
- Purchasing

Instructional Posters
(purchased or created)
- Money
- Shapes
- Fractions
- Measurement
- Times table
- Etc.

Manipulatives
- Hundreds, tens, and ones
- Counters
- Unifix cubes
- Etc.

Ruler
- Measurement
- Inches and centimeters

Thermometer
(manipulative)

Clock
(manipulative)

Geometric Forms and Shapes

Resources:

- ☐ Number chart
- ☐ Chart paper
- ☐ Instructional posters
- ☐ Manipulatives
- ☐ Ruler
- ☐ Geometric forms and shapes
- ☐ Clock
- ☐ Thermometer
- ☐ Money manipulatives
- ☐ Flash cards

Manipulatives

Manipulatives are tangible items that can be used as instructional math aides. They offer a visual, hands-on approach to learning. Some students need manipulatives to solidify concepts, and all students can benefit from their use. It is important to give students free exploration time with a manipulative as they are introduced. Getting the playing out of the way enables students to focus and use the manipulatives as a tool. With time, they become less and less of a distraction. You may bag up manipulatives for easy distribution and collection. You may even prepare manipulatives bags for each student with a collection of commonly used manipulatives for easy access. These bags can be kept in their table boxes. Manipulatives are more common in lower grades but are helpful even with upper-grade concepts. You can even create your own manipulatives with common objects such as beans, buttons, bottle caps, etc. Send a letter home and invite students to bring in items.

Container Options

| Plastic Candy Container | Plastic Jar | Shoe Box | Cut-and-Taped Water Container |

65
© The McGraw-Hill Companies, Inc.

Manipulatives Use Guide

Beans
- Counting
- Sorting
- ±
- Tens/ones sticks
- Graphing

Counters
- ±
- Numbers chart
- Probability

Money
- Counting $
- ± $
- Buying
- Probability

Bears (animals)
- Counting
- Sorting
- ±
- Graphing

Dice
- Probability
- ±

Tangrams
- Shapes
- Geometry
- Puzzles

Blocks or Cubes
- Counting
- Sorting
- ±
- Graphing

Forms
- Geometry
- Volume

Quisinar Rods
(tens/ones)
- Counting hundreds, tens, ones
- Double digit
- ±
- Regrouping

Buttons
- Counting
- Sorting
- ±
- Graphing

Geo Boards
- Geometry
- Shapes
- Angles
- Sides

Unifix Cubes
- Counting
- Sorting
- ±
- Graphing
- Measurement

Clock
- Telling time

Links
- Counting
- Sorting
- ±
- Graphing

Dominoes
- Counting
- ±
- Grouping
- Sorting

66

Websites for Teachers

The Internet is an *excellent* resource for both you and your students. The best way to find sites is to surf the Web. Sites have links to other websites, and you can spend hours discovering valuable resources. Find what works for you and bookmark those sites into a teacher folder. Ask other teachers which websites they use. From lesson plans to great art ideas, the Internet is the best overall resource you can use. This is a list of some great teacher websites. Try these and add your own.

Website	Description
teachers.net	General resource
echantedlearning.com	General resource
schooldiscovery.com	Resource/links
orientaltrading.com	Arts and crafts supplies
edhelper.com	Excellent resource, holidays/graphic organizers, curriculum
sitesforteachers.com	Excellent source of links
teacherplanet.com	Calendar of events/lessons/ideas
grantsalert.com	Grants
rubistar.4teachers.org	Rubrics
mysimon.com	Pricing for grants
techlearning.com	Grants

Websites for Students

The internet is an *excellent* resource for both you and your students. Always preview sites prior to allowing students to use them. Most schools or districts have a firewall (a barrier that is set up to block inappropriate sites), but it is your responsibility to know what your students are looking at. The following is a list of websites that students can utilize. Check them out and see what works for you; add new ones to the list. Again, ask other teachers at your grade level what they use. Inquire about any district- or school-approved website lists.

Website	Description
cybersleuth-kids.com	Internet search guide for kids
kidzone.ws	Learning facts
ajkids.com	Question search
yahooligans.yahoo.com	Web guide for kids
theartgallery.com.au	Kid art
ala.org	American Library Association, links
kidsdomain.com	Resource/links
kidsread.com	Reading resource, books to games
enviroliteracy.org	Science websites
science.howstuffworks.com	Science resource
kidsclick.org	Resource
coolmath4kids.com	Math resource
funbrain.com/kidscenter.html	Resource/games
pbskids.org	Resource

The School

Ten Teacher Reminders

Teachers are faced with many challenges today, especially with legalities that can be easily avoided. This suggested list of reminders is very important to consider in this profession to avoid potential problems. Know your school or district policies, and always ask other teachers and/or your union representative. In many instances, just using common sense will go a long way.

1. *Never* stay alone with a student behind closed doors. Always have the doors open and, better yet, have other students around.

2. *Never* photograph or digitally record your students for use outside of the classroom without a signed legal consent form from the parent/guardian. Your school or district should have a standard release form. Ask how others handle this.

3. Be very careful with any snacks you have in the classroom. Students may have allergies. Peanuts, dairy products, and so on can all cause reactions. Know your students!

4. *Never* strike or aggressively grab a student. Any contact, depending on your rapport and the student, can be misconstrued into something it is not.

5. *Never* leave your school site with any student without a signed permission slip and their emergency contact information. Your school should have a standard trip slip form. Ask.

6. *Never* release a student to anyone without an official school release from the office. The office has a list of approved individuals that students can be released to.

7. Always document student referrals to the office for behavior or health issues. Cover yourself. Save all such documentation.

8. *Never* solicit funds or donations without first checking your school or district policy and protocol. Always ask first to cover yourself.

9. Get to know your union representative and union rights. Union reps can be helpful in answering contract questions and are an excellent resource. You may need their support one day.

10. *Never* let your credentials expire. Stay on top of what you need to do to stay current. This is your job! It is your responsibility and can easily be neglected. Don't get caught—be proactive.

Procedures for Bathroom, Nurse, and Office

This is a very simple page designed with reminders about sending students out of the room. These ideas apply to kindergarten through fifth grade but are good ideas for every grade level up through twelfth. Remember to check your school's guidelines in case there are other requirements for students leaving the room.

Reminders

1. In the lower grades (K–5) always send children in pairs. (For the restroom, boys with boys and girls with girls)

2. Always send students with a hall pass. If students are going to the nurse or the office, a note may also be required.

3. If students are going to the restroom, remind them to wash their hands. Even students in the upper grades can use this reminder.

Library Visits

School libraries are a fantastic resource. Many schools have a librarian and/or library aide trained to facilitate your visits and book checkouts. These visits not only provide you with a break from the classroom routine but lay the foundation for your students to make books a consistent part of their lives as well. These visits also help them learn valuable research skills.

You need to find out:

- if the library is available.
- what the sign-up policy is.
- whether there are scheduled days or times.
- what the librarian's or aide's name is.

Library Hints and Considerations:

- Review library rules (obtain from the library or use generic rules listed).
  - No food or drink in the library
  - Use inside voices.
  - Follow directions.
  - Preview one book at a time.
  - Use a marker to save book's location.
  - Shelve books with the spine facing out.
  - If you are unsure of a book's location, leave for the librarian or teacher to reshelve.

- Review the parts of a book.

Front cover

Spine

by Sarah Chase
Illustrated by Ron Smith

Author

Illustrator

Table of contents

Copyright
Publisher

Back cover

Book synopsis

Author's bio

- Review types of books and their uses.
  - Fiction
  - Nonfiction
  - Expository
  - Historical

- Create student markers.

- Review library policy and procedure.
  - Checkout-card information (name, class, date, title, due date)
  - Checkout time limit
  - Lost or damaged book policy

Computer Lab Visits

Many schools have computer labs that classrooms visit on a rotating schedule. There may be a full-time computer teacher and/or lab aide with a set curriculum of lessons that they follow. This is a critical part of any student's education and should be fully taken advantage of.

You need to find out:

if a computer lab is operational.

what grades utilize the lab.

whether the lab is on a sign-up basis.

what the scheduled days or times are.

what students will do in the lab.

what your role is in the lab.

Computer Lab Hints and Considerations:

- Review computer lab rules (lab rules or generic rules listed).
  - No food or drink in the lab
  - Do not operate computer until instructed to do so.
  - Follow directions.
  - Stay only on assigned task.

- Review computer etiquette and usage.
  - Use with care.
  - Shut down properly.
  - Never disassemble or insert foreign objects.
  - Never disconnect cables or any external hardware.

- Establish lab buddy partners.
  - Group high to medium and medium to low.
  - Keep in mind that computer skills don't directly correlate to academic performance.

- Surf the Internet for websites that your students can browse related to current theme.
  - Always be prepared to go it alone in case there is no assigned teacher and/or aide.
  - Always have a list of approved websites for students to visit.

Fire Drills, Earthquakes, and Emergencies

Any time there is an emergency, you should have some type of plan established with your class. When you are in charge of a group of students, it's important to have this emergency plan well rehearsed. Your school and school district should have developed plans for emergencies already in place. However, if you're not sure about what to do in an emergency, check with your administration for procedures and plans for emergencies. Being prepared for an emergency is essential when moving students to safety, and it can save lives. Along with your school plan, you should have an established plan within your classroom as well. These are a few ideas to help in your preparation.

- Have an emergency kit in your classroom. This kit should be in plain sight and easy to grab in an emergency. The contents should be checked and updated every six months. Check the following page for items your emergency kit should contain.

- Develop an emergency signal or a code word that your class will respond to immediately. This signal can be specific to your class—a clap, a bell, and a word phrase.

- Develop an ordered plan of actions your class will follow in response to the emergency signal. For example, when the emergency signal is given, they should put their hands on their head, turn their eyes on you, and listen for directions.

- Establish a partnership with another teacher next door or across the hall. If one of you were not able to respond in an emergency, your partner could get students to safety.

- Be safe, and practice once a month.

Classroom Emergency Supplies

Item	Quantity
Adhesive Tape	1 roll
Ammonia Inhalants	5
Backpack/Duffel Bag	1
Bandages	1 box
Batteries	4
Cold Packs	2 packs
First-Aid Handbook	1
Flashlight	1
Gum	2 packages
Hydrogen Peroxide	1 bottle
Ibuprofen/Tylenol	1 bottle
Latex Gloves	10 pairs
Life Savers (candy)	2 packages
Light Stick	2
Pad of Paper	1 pad
Paper Cups	1 bag
Pen	1
Pencil	1
Premoistened Towelettes	1 package
Resealable Bags	1 box
Roller Bandage—3"	1
Safety Pins	1 package
Saline Solution	1
Sanitary Napkins	1 box
Scissors	1 pair
Sewing Kit	1
Solar Blanket	1
Toilet Paper	2 rolls
Trash Bags	1 box
Tums	1 pack
Tweezers	1 pair
Water	1 bottle
Waterproof Matches	1 box
Whistle	1

75

Use this form to document the change in location of a student to another classroom (e.g., if left behind on a field trip with no consent form).

Temporary Student Displacement Form

Date: _____ Grade: _____ Room: _____ Teacher: _____

Reason for Displacement:

☐ Field trip-—student has no written consent.

☐ Activity exclusion due to: _____ health _____ religion _____ other (_____)

Student's Name	Room Number	Teacher	Additional Information
1.			
2.			
3.			
4.			
5.			
6.			

Temporary Student Displacement Form

Date: _____ Grade: _____ Room: _____ Teacher: _____

Reason for Displacement:

☐ Field trip—student has no written consent.

☐ Activity exclusion due to: _____ health _____ religion _____ other (_____)

Student's Name	Room Number	Teacher	Additional Information
1.			
2.			
3.			
4.			
5.			
6.			

Record Keeping

Item Name	Serial Number	Quantity

Professional Records

Y ou should always maintain evidence of your personal professional growth records, trainings, and classes. These not only create a portfolio but also may serve as necessary documentation for credential renewal, depending on your state's credentialing guidelines and renewal policy. Maintaining a professional file of all such documentation is highly recommended and saves time if and when you need such documentation.

You should save:

Certificates
- Course completions
- Recognitions

Agendas
- Professional developments
- All trainings

Current Professional Résumé

Letters of Recommendation

Professional Trainings

University Transcripts

Records and Documentation

Photographs of:
- Classroom
- Bulletin boards
- Centers
- Student projects

Performance Evaluations

Observations of Yourself

Sample Lesson Plans
- Weekly
- Long-term or annual
- Unit or theme

School-Year Inventory

The following is an overview of possible paperwork, record keeping, and assessments that your school or district may require. Half the battle is staying up to date on this.

Beginning of the Year

- ☐ **Enrollment** _____ Boys _____ Girls
- ☐ **Emergency Contact Information Cards** (Check about school procedures—usually kept in office.)
- ☐ **Open Formal Records** (Check with school for format and procedures.)
- ☐ **School Paperwork** (Check with school for release paperwork, compacts, government-funded forms, etc.)
- ☐ **Evaluation Paperwork** (Some schools may have you submit professional goals and long-term plans prior to a formal evaluation. Check for sign-up procedures, available dates, person evaluating you, subject observed.)
- ☐ **Substitute Folder** (Some schools require general information turned in for subs or emergency plans for up to three days.)
- ☐ **Initial Assessments** (personal assessments, schoolwide assessments, e.g., assessments for funding programs)
- ☐ **Portfolios and Assessment Folders** (Establish and have initial samples in first few days of school.)

Middle of the Year

- ☐ **Assessments** (Check school for district assessment schedule. Conduct personal midyear evaluation. Some districts conduct six-week assessments in Math and Reading.)
- ☐ **Ongoing Record Keeping** (Some districts have you complete and submit a monthly attendance evaluation or register.)
- ☐ **Formal Evaluations** (Check to see if you are being evaluated, on what subject, with what expectations. Set up dates for formal evaluation(s) and check how many informal evaluations will be conducted.)

End of the Year

- ☐ **Close formal records or retentions.** (Check with school for procedures and due dates.)
- ☐ **Reorganize class for placement.** (Some schools have reorganizations, where each teacher divides his or her class into boys and girls, ability levels, behavior, and language levels. Classes are created to meet student needs.)
- ☐ **Inventory room equipment.** (List name and serial numbers for all equipment.)
- ☐ **Return all textbooks and library books.** (Inventory against bar code and return.)
- ☐ **Submit all attendance records.** (Ink in with *black* ink over any pencil.)

Attendance

Good attendance is essential to great teaching. Depending on where you teach, attendance may be easy, or it could be a lot of work. Wherever you are, having a class with great attendance makes your job easier and the students learn better. While students are required usually by state laws to be at school, this isn't an "end all, cure all." You will always have students who never miss a day, but what can be done about those few students who just aren't getting to school? If you are looking for some ideas to improve your attendance, you've come to the right place.

☐ Be diligent with your record keeping! Take attendance every day. Attendance cards are usually legal documents that require your attention and accuracy.

☐ Establish a system of rewards or incentives for perfect attendance.

- Give a weekly award.
- Give a monthly award.
- Give an end-of-the-year award.

☐ If an absence occurs, try to call home on the day missed. Although this is usually not required, calling home is a great way to get students back to school and lets the parents know you care!

☐ Get acquainted with your district and school attendance policies.

☐ Report outstanding absences. If a student is absent for more than a few days, it's a good idea to bring this to the attention of an administrator or your school counselor.

Teacher: _____   Room Number: _____   Year: _____

Student's Name	Address	Phone Number	E-mail Address

Teacher: _____ **Room Number:** _____ **Year:** _____

Student's Name NAMES	Birthday	Phone Number
1.		
2.		
3.		
4.		
5.		
6.		
7.		
8.		
9.		
10.		
11.		
12.		
13.		
14.		
15.		
16.		
17.		
18.		
19.		
20.		
21.		
22.		
23.		
24.		
25.		
26.		
27.		
28.		
29.		
30.		

Cumulative Records

Most school districts have some sort of cumulative record that follows a student from prekindergarten or kindergarten through the twelfth grade. These records are legal documents that contain a student's scholastic history. Depending on your district, this information may be in a hard-copy file format or may be input into a computer. Information may vary, and it is important to familiarize yourself with what information is recorded. The beginning of the school year is an excellent time to open these records, inputting students' most recent information. It is also an opportunity for you to get to know your students, their scholastic history, and any special services and/or needs they may have.

You need to find out:

- **if the school or district has cumulative student records.**

- **if records are hard-copy files. How are they accessed?**
  (location, available times, contact person, school checkout policy)

- **if the records are electronic computer files. How are they accessed?**
  (URL/website, computers [school or home, necessary passwords])

- **what the school or district policies and dates are.**

- **what the opening date is.** (opening information/procedure)

- **what the closing date is.** (closing information, procedure, deadline)

- **what is housed in these records.**
  - Special services documentation
  - Health records
  - Intervention records
  - Report cards
  - Student study team records
  - Language records
  - Standardized test scores
  - State/federally funded program information
  - Evaluations and testing results
  - Annual photographs

Possible Student Information:
- Student's ID number
- Student's date of birth
- Current address and phone number
- Dates of enrollment—entered and exited (e.g., "E")
- Special codes for entrances and exits (e.g., "E-2")
- Attendance (present, absent, tardies)
- Teacher
- Picture

Possible Curricular Information:
- Text series, publisher, edition
- Reading, Science, Social Science

Possible Scholastic Information:
- Teacher's initials and grade
- Teacher's comments
- Conference or meeting dates and attendees
- Standardized test scores

Possible Additional Records:
- Special services
- Interventions
- Language
- Health records

Report-Card Checklist

Several times a year, teachers will formally record the progress of their students. This is an excellent opportunity to focus on each student and his or her progress. It is very important for your students, too. It is important that you be well prepared with evidence to support your scores. Ongoing work sample collections from a portfolio and a work folder can be helpful. Additionally, it is nice to use a quick one-on-one assessment inventory in Math and Reading to confirm each student's progress and to clarify your observations.

Needed information:

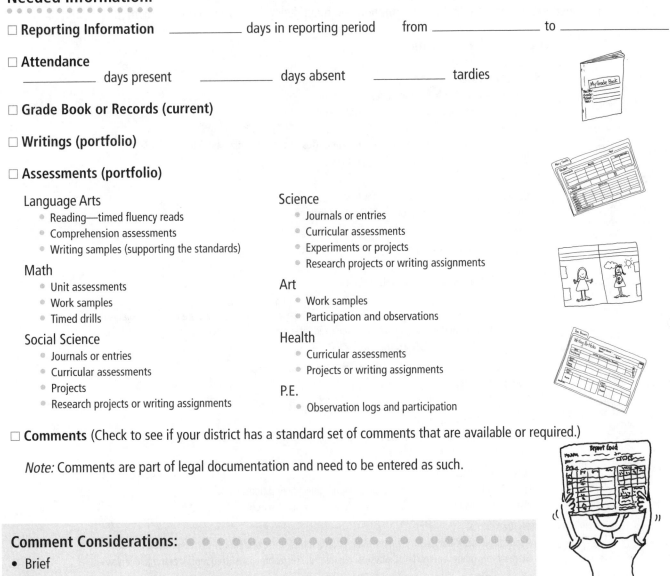

☐ **Reporting Information** _____ days in reporting period   from _____ to _____

☐ **Attendance**
_____ days present   _____ days absent   _____ tardies

☐ **Grade Book or Records (current)**

☐ **Writings (portfolio)**

☐ **Assessments (portfolio)**

Language Arts
- Reading—timed fluency reads
- Comprehension assessments
- Writing samples (supporting the standards)

Math
- Unit assessments
- Work samples
- Timed drills

Social Science
- Journals or entries
- Curricular assessments
- Projects
- Research projects or writing assignments

Science
- Journals or entries
- Curricular assessments
- Experiments or projects
- Research projects or writing assignments

Art
- Work samples
- Participation and observations

Health
- Curricular assessments
- Projects or writing assignments

P.E.
- Observation logs and participation

☐ **Comments** (Check to see if your district has a standard set of comments that are available or required.)

Note: Comments are part of legal documentation and need to be entered as such.

Comment Considerations:
- Brief
- Professional
- Positive (Try to always find the positive, nice way to end your comments.)
- Nondiagnostic (ADD, ADHD, etc. can only be diagnosed by a doctor or a licensed psychologist.)
- Nonaccusatory (Avoid direct accusations, e.g., "Sam hits children on the yard" is better stated "Sam has a hard time maintaining his hands and feet to himself when in the yard.")

Student Referrals

Sometimes it is necessary to seek additional assistance for a student who has special circumstances beyond your capabilities. It is important to exhaust your resources first and to document every intervention. This documentation of behavior will greatly assist any professional handling the student's case. *Never* diagnose a student's issue, even if it seems obvious. A professional needs to conduct a formal evaluation, and it must go through the proper channels. Only report what you see and what you have tried to do to assist your student in need. Always check with your school or district about referral procedures and your responsibilities in the process. Some schools may have a team of professionals that handles the referrals.

You need to be prepared, and the information you need depends on your school or district.

Needed information:

☐ **Student's Information**

- Name/student ID (where applicable)
- Date of birth/current age
- Current address
- Parent/guardian's name and home environment (foster care, guardianship, etc.)
- Primary language (if applicable) ELD level: _____

☐ **Attendance**
- Current year's: absences: _____ tardies: _____
- Previous years' (down to kindergarten) attendance
- Suspensions _____

☐ **Description of Concern**
- Academic
- Attendance
- Emotional/behavioral
- Speech
- Other

In a paragraph, describe your concerns. Do so in an objective manner. Simply state the facts—facts that you can support with documentation and attempted interventions.

☐ **Parental/Guardian Notification**
- Notified/conferenced with parent/guardian on several occasions
- About concern(s)
- Notified parent/guardian about referral and referral procedures

☐ **Academic Information**

- Current assessments in Math and Reading
- Other assessments or inventories

☐ **Health Information**
- List of any known health issues (eyeglasses, diagnosed conditions, etc.)
- List of any current known medications child is receiving at school

☐ **Observations**
- Academic—work habits, motivation, subject difficulties, understanding, attention, focus
- Medical—hygiene, energy level, physical complaints, restroom visits (frequency), asthma, eyeglasses, etc.
- Behavioral—withdrawn, violent, depressed or sad, temperamental, aggressive, disruptive, immature

☐ **Interventions**

- Teaching Modifications—positive feedback, visual aids, peer or cross-age tutoring, reteaching, small-group instruction, individual instruction, goals, contracts
- Teaching Accommodations—seating adjustments, changing classes
- Teaching Materials—remedial work or less work, manipulatives, books on tape, graphic organizers, blocking text or color coding

Student's Name: _____

TIME AND DATE	BEHAVIOR

Retention Checklist

Retention is a critical decision that has a tremendous impact on a student's life. It is a last resort only after all other options have not yielded the results necessary to bring him or her academically to grade level. The goal of a retention is for the student to have an opportunity to mature and grow academically to grade level and even beyond. In the right situation, the student can flourish and gain confidence. It can be harder on older students who tend to be more aware of how a retention can be perceived. The teacher plays a critical role in such a transition and needs to be positive and sensitive. This is not a quick fix but a calculated move. A retention can be a lost year if a student is not qualified, and it should never be taken lightly. Because of this, a number of criteria need to be considered prior to making a retention. Start by checking with your school or district for specific qualifications and age cut-offs. Ask other teachers when a student should be considered for retention. Keep in mind that the student's parent/guardian always has the final approval.

The information you need depends on your school or district.

Needed information:

☐ **Student's Information**
- Name/student ID (where applicable)
- Date of birth, current age, and age entering sixth grade if retained
- Current address
- Parent/guardian's name and home environment (foster care, guardianship, etc.)
- Primary language (if applicable) ELD level: _____
- Attendance
- Current grade: _____ days absent (_____ excused/_____ unexcused)
  Previous:

  _____ Grade: _____ days absent (_____ excused/_____ unexcused)
  _____ Grade: _____ days absent (_____ excused/_____ unexcused)
  _____ Grade: _____ days absent (_____ excused/_____ unexcused)

☐ **Reason for Retention**
- Write a statement that specifically states why you feel student needs to be retained. This statement should not be diagnostic but be based on your observations.

☐ **Parental/Guardian Notification or Request**
- Notification on report card (Some districts have a warning notification check-off.)
- Notification/discussion of potential at conferences (Note dates of each conference and participants.)
- Notification specifically for submission and request ("May be retained.")
- Parent/guardian request for retention: _____ Written _____ Oral _____ Date(s)

☐ **Consultation with Previous Teacher/Student's Cumulative Record**
- Discuss observations and academic performance.
- Check for documented support and possible explanations.

☐ **Health Status**
- Check with school nurse.
- Consult records for any health issues or medications that should be considered.
- Physical size in present grade: Small   Medium   Large

☐ **Academic Records**
- Standardized test scores: _____ Reading _____ Math _____ Language

☐ **Referral Services**
- Special services received:
  - Reading resource
  - Speech
  - Adaptive P.E.
  - Other

☐ **Agency Support**
- Outside agency support

☐ **Referral for Evaluation**
- Reason (if different from retention)
- Evaluation committee
  _____ Administrator _____ Teacher _____ Parent/Guardian _____ Student _____ Psychologist _____ Counselor
  _____ Outreach Consultant _____ Social Worker _____ Speech Therapist _____ Reading Resource
- Date
- Recommendation

Follow-up may include:

- school administrator approval/"OK" = "will be retained."
- school or district letter to parent/guardian.
- notation in student's cumulative record. (Check for documentation procedure.)
- notation on final report card.

Curriculum

Mr. Stewart

Grade 3

Unit Plan

Reading
* Picture Books
  - I See Indians
  - Look at Tribes
* S.S text pages

P.E.
* Culture games
  - capture-the-feather
  - tribal games

Social Studies
- Money systems
- History of Tribes
  - Seminoles
  - Chicktaw

Vocabulary
- Tribes   - Artifacts
- Foods   - Tools
- Materials   - Names

Theme:
Native Americans
5-6 weeks

Science
- Food
- Making Fire
- Fishing Methods

Field Trips
- Missions
- Local Tribes
- Histnic Places

Art
- Artifacts   - Jewelry
- Pictures   - Clothing
- Tribal Headware

Math
* Timeline
  - Indian Flourished
    + Decline
* Graphs & Tally

Technology
- Indian Web-sites
- Indian research sites.

Music
* Traditional Songs
  - Indian Chant
* Traditional Instruments
  - Drums   - Rython
  - Voice   - Song

Language-Arts Overview

Spelling Patterns

Consonants: b, c, d, f, g, h, . . .

Vowels: a, e, i, o, u

Short Vowels: **a**pple, **e**gg, **i**gloo, **o**ctopus, **u**mbrella

Long Vowels: **a**pe, **e**normous, **i**ce, **o**at, **u**nicorn

Long A	Long E	Long I	Long O	Long U
b**a**ke	m**e**	K**i**nd	n**o**	**u**nicorn
p**ai**l	P**e**te	b**i**ke	j**o**ke	m**u**le
acorn	F**ee**t	cr**y**	b**oa**t	h**ue**
d**ay**	S**ea**t	h**igh**	t**oe**	f**ew**
	Ch**ie**f	t**ie**	sh**ow**	
	Cit**y**			

C = consonant

V = vowel

VC word = at

CV word = go

CVC word = cat

CVCC word = back

Sight Words = high-frequency words, sometimes nondecodable words: I, me, was, were, from, make, etc.

Vowels

Vowel Digraphs: Two letters (vowels) ½ that together make one sound: **ai**, **ay**, **oa**, **oe**, **ow**, **ee**, **ey**, **ea**, **ie**, **ei**.

Vowel Dipthongs: Two vowels that together make a new, special sound: **au**, **aw**, **oi**, **oy**, **oo**, **eu**, **ue**, **ew**, **ui**, **ou**, **ow**.

R-Controlled Vowel Sounds: Vowels followed by *r* that create a new sound: **ar**, **er**, **ir**, **ur**, **or**.

The Letter Y: *Y* has the sound of a long *i* at the end of one-syllable words: cr**y**, m**y**, fl**y**; *y* has the sound of long *e* at the end of words with two or more syllables: cit**y**, prett**y**, rub**y**.

The Letter W: *W* can make an *a* have a short *o* sound: **wa**sh, **wa**tch, s**wa**t.

The Letters QU: *Qu* can also make an *a* have a short *o* sound (*qu* is pronounced "kwah," like it has a *w*): s**qua**t, **qua**drant.

Consonants

Two-Sounded Consonants: (1) *G* and *c* can be hard or soft.
soft *c* = **c**ent, **c**ircle, **c**ytoplasm; hard *c* = **c**at, magi**c**, s**c**an
soft *g* = **g**entle, **g**iraffe, **g**ym; hard *g* = **g**um, ba**g**, **g**rape
(2) *S* can make an *s* and *z* sound.
   s = **s**: **s**ee, pa**ss**
   s = **z**: bee**s**, lo**s**e

The Letters X and Q: These consonants have the sounds of two consonants combined: *x* = "ks"; *q* = "kw."

Silent Consonants: These are two consonants with one silent letter: **kn**ight, **wr**ite, **rh**yme, co**mb**, autu**mn**, ni**gh**t.

Consonant Blends: These are two consonants blended in which you hear a little of each consonant.
   L blends: **bl**, **cl**, **fl**, **gl**, **pl**, **sl**.
   S blends: **sm**, **sn**, **sk**, **sc**, **st**, **sp**, **sw**, **str**, **spr**, **spl**, **scr**.
   R blends: **br**, **cr**, **dr**, **fr**, **gr**, **pr**, **tr**.

Consonant Digraphs: Two consonants come together to make one new sound: **sh**ip, **ch**in, ba**ck**, **ph**oto, **th**in, **wh**ip, lau**gh**.

The Writing Process and Stages

The Writing Process

Prewrite
- Ideas on paper
- Graphic organizers

Draft
- Write it all down.
- Notes to main idea/details
- "No Worry" writing

Edit and Revise
- Check for clarity and content.
- Add or change information.

Proofread
- Check grammar and spelling.
- Check mechanics.

Publish
- Create final draft.
- "My best"

Share and Reflect
- Display
- Share
- Discuss

Writing Stages

Precommunicative
- Pictures, attempts, letters

Semiphonetic
- Initial consonants to initial and final

I sau detm
W pla n d prk

Phonetic
- Vowels and syllables represented

I lik to swim n d osun

The elafant ran in the jungul.

Transitional
- Sentences with correct spelling emerging

I went to the park to play
Wit mi frend. We playd on
the slide and we playd ball.
It wuz fun to play.

Conventional Spelling
- Standard spelling and writing

Types of Writing

Independent Writing: Independent, variety of forms and purposes (journals, labeling, student books, etc.)

Interactive Writing: With teacher or class, students plan or write together as a group; taking turns, models, supports phonics (whole-class story).

Shared Writing: Teacher writes, students compose, copy, or transcribe.

Guided Writing (writer's workshop): Teacher or small group write together; a community of writers.

Basic Grammar and Punctuation

Grammar

Part of Speech	Definition	Example
Noun	A person, place, or thing	**Tom** (person) sat on the **bench** (thing) in the **park** (place).
Pronoun	Takes the place of a noun	Mary is my friend. **She** is tall. (I, he, she, it, we, you, they) Sam's dog is big. **His** dog is big. (my, his, her, me, its, our, your, their)
Adjective	Describes a noun	The man sat. The **large**, **old** man sat.
Verb	An action word	The stallion **runs** fast.
Adverb	Describes a verb	The tortoise walks **slowly**.
Preposition	Relates nouns or pronouns to other words	The frog jumped **into** the pond.
Conjunction	Joins words, phrases, or clauses	Sam read **and** Jan wrote a story.

Punctuation

Period (.): ends a telling sentence: *The horse eats hay.*

Question Mark (?): ends a question: *What color is the horse?*

Exclamation Mark (!): ends an exclamation: *The barn is on fire!*

Quotation Marks ("/"): around a quote: *He said, "The horse is white."*

Comma (,): gives pause or is used in a series: *"Next time, use . . ."; red, blue, green.*

Semicolon (;): separates two sentences that are closely related: *My family is Jewish; we celebrate Passover but not Easter.*

Colon (:): precedes a list or greeting part of a business letter or indicates dialogue: *You need: a bag, . . .; Dear sir:*

Hyphen (-): unifies words, prefixes, numbers: *city-state, half-asleep, twenty-two*

Apostrophe ('): possessives, contractions: *Sarah's cat, don't*

Writing Genres

Narrative Writing

- Tells a story
- Gives an account

Uses: imagination, personal accounts

Written in first or third person (I, we/he, she, it, they)

Expository Writing

- Explains or defines
- Gives information

Uses: facts, statistical information, cause and effect, examples

Written in third person (he, she it, they)

Descriptive Writing

- Describes
- Is useful in all writing

Uses: descriptive language, adjectives

Written in first or third person; shows, doesn't tell

Summary Writing

- Summarizes
- Maintains integrity of original document

Uses: main ideas, events, concepts

Written in first or third person

Response to Literature

- Reaction or response to literature
- Personal connection to writer's ideas or experiences

Uses: meaning

Written by retelling, summarizing, analyzing, and/or generalizing

Poetry Writing

- Arranged composition

Uses: sound and rhythm

Written types: haiku, cinquain, limericks, concrete, closed verse, lyric, nonsense verse, narrative, jump rope

Report Writing

- Explains and informs
- Gives information and facts

Uses: to educate, report facts, predict based on data

Letter Writing

- Friendly, formal, or business
- Conveys or shares information

Friendly Letter Parts

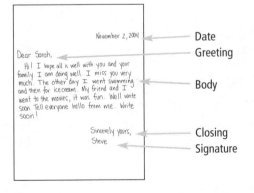

November 2, 2004	Date
Dear Sarah,	Greeting
Hi! I hope all is well with you and your family. I am doing well. I miss you very much. The other day I went swimming and then for ice cream. My friend and I went to the movies, it was fun. We'll write soon. Tell everyone hello from me. Write soon!	Body
Sincerely yours, Steve	Closing Signature

Business Letter Parts

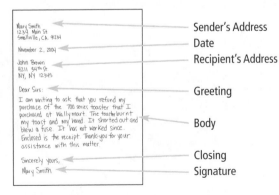

Mary Smith 1234 Main St. Smallville, CA. 91234	Sender's Address
November 2, 2004	Date
John Brown 4211 34th St. NY, NY 12345	Recipient's Address
Dear Sirs:	Greeting
I am writing to ask that you refund my purchase of the 700 series toaster that I purchased at Wally mart. The toaster burnt my toast and my hand. It shorted out and blew a fuse. It has not worked since. Enclosed is the receipt. Thank you for your assistance with this matter.	Body
Sincerely yours, Mary Smith	Closing Signature

Ways to Write

First Person: **I**   Second Person: **you**   Third Person: **he, she, they**

Proofreading Marks

Correction	Symbol	Example
Capitalize.	≡	<u>a</u> dog ran in the park.
Add punctuation marks.	⊙	Where are you going⑦
Add word(s).	⋀	My ∧^bike is red.
Delete word(s).	ℓ	Her mother is of nice.
Check spelling.	◯	When did you ⟨leaf⟩?
Indent paragraph.	¶	¶ The morning I woke with a cold…
Change to lowercase.	/	My family Is going to the park.
Reverse.	∼	The shorts blue are dirty.

Reading Genres

Realistic Fiction
- Takes place in modern time
- Here and now
- Realistic events

Mystery
- Mysterious event(s)
- Explained or revealed at the end of the book
- Suspenseful

Poetry
- Verse
- Creates thoughts or feelings
- Rhythm and rhyme

Historical Fiction
- Made-up
- Pertains to time in past
- Setting real, characters fictional

Folktale
- No known author
- Passed from generation to generation

Nonfiction
- True facts
- Any subject
- About people = biography

Drama
- Written to act out
- Audience

Myth
- Explains something
- Gods or superhumans

Biography
- Story of a person's life
- Told by another person

Autobiography
- Story of a person's life
- Told by that person

Science Fiction
- Blends scientific fact and fiction
- Futuristic technology

Many of the above-mentioned genres can be found as picture books. A *picture book* is a book in which the illustrations play a significant role in telling the story. Traditionally, picture books are approximately thirty-two-page books. Occasionally a picture book will exceed the traditional length, and these are usually geared toward the upper end of the age spectrum. Picture books cover a wide range of topics and styles.

Ways to Read

Choral Reading

- "Unison reading"
- Many opportunities for repeated readings of a selected piece
- Practice in oral reading
- Excellent for poetry or rhymes
- Repeated readings of big books

Shared Reading

- Teacher reads a big book or text.
- Students view or follow.
- Early reading strategies
- Phonemic awareness
- Model reading strategies
- Predicting
- Use of contextual clues

Read Aloud

- Teacher reads to class.
- Class discussion and dialogue
- Follow-up activity: journals, art, etc.
- Pure enjoyment (Teacher doesn't stop to summarize or ask questions.)

Popcorn Reading

- Teacher asks students to begin reading aloud.
- Any willing student can start.
- When student stops, another student continues (without teacher's direction).
- Continues until all have read
- Builds responsibility to participate and gives a choice of when to do so
- Lower-grade students can pick next reader who has not read yet.

Timed Reading

- Designated number of minutes
- Student reads twice.
- Attempt to read further the second time
- Number of words/minute
- Builds fluency

Buddy Reading

- Students pair up.
- Lower-grade student pairs with upper-grade student.
- Students read and discuss the story.
- Students take turns reading aloud.
- Older student serves as coach or reading mentor.

Partner Reading

- Students in a class pair up.
- Take turns and assist one another
- Showcases their skills
- Select special spot to read in the room
- Can pair high/medium and medium/low or allow students to select

Independent Reading

- Students read independently.
- Practice learned strategies
- Builds fluency
- Problem-solving application

Sustained Silent Reading (SSR)

- Students read.
- Independent and silent
- Individual instructional levels
- Provides practice
- Encourages reading
- Uninterrupted sustained silent reading (USSR)
- Drop everything and read (DEAR)

Guided Reading

- Teacher and student read text together.
- Teacher and student read, think, and talk through text.
- Supports intervention
- Teaches problem solving
- Can also "echo read" (teacher reads and students reread)

Comprehension

Author Considerations

Author's Point of View

- Who is telling the story?
- First person: I, me, my
- Third person: he/she, him/her, they/them

Author's Purpose

- To entertain
- To explain
- To inform
- To persuade

Good Reader Considerations

Main Ideas and Details

- What is the primary focus of the story?

Compar d Contrast

- Find similarities and differences.

Cause and Effect

- What took place (problem)?
- What were the outcomes (solution)?

Classify or Categorize

- Sort story elements into similar groups.

Opinion and Fact

- Feeling vs. real

Shared Reading

- Predict, infer, make assumptions, discover author's meaning.

Make Connections

- Relate to a personal experience.

Math Overview

Mathematics is a very important part of a child's education. It is taught sequentially, aligning to the developmentally age-appropriate skills and concepts. In other words, students are introduced to skills that they are ready for and that lay the foundation for consecutive higher-level skills to be introduced in subsequent grade levels. The following is an overview or breakdown of the basic math strands taught for each grade level. This is just a glimpse of what each grade level looks like at each strand, which can vary from state to state. As with all curricular areas, consult your state standards and your state or district's adopted curriculum. The major strands are as follows.

Number Sense

Number sense is gaining an understanding of numbers, their relationships, and what they represent.

Teaching Tips:

- Manipulatives are excellent for building number sense.
- Hundreds chart and number line are excellent tools.
  - Counting and counting patterns—one more/one less, ten more/ten less, etc.
  - Counting on and counting back to $\pm$

Measurement/Geometry

Measurement involves length, volume, and weight. Geometry deals with shapes and solids, their characteristics, and their area/perimeter.

Teaching Tips:

- Solids or shape manipulatives are excellent tools.
- Measure something every day; repetition builds mastery.
- Set up a center for measurement and volumes.

$A = a^3$

Algebra

Algebra involves solving mathematical problems through interpretations and properties.

Teaching Tips:

- "Problem a day" with whole class

$$3 + \_ = 7 \qquad 3n + 2 = 14$$
$$3n = 12$$
$$n = 4$$

Heads
|||
Tails
卌

Statistics, Data Analysis, and Probability

Involves analyzing, comparing, and interpreting data; prediction and probability.

Teaching Tips:

- Manipulatives with graphing grids or mats
- Coin tossing or dice rolling

Mathematical Reasoning

3+4=7
so
7-4=3

Explaining approach and solution, application to other problems

Teaching Tips:

- "Problem a day" with whole class
- Math journals

Number Sense

Kindergarten

Numbers 1 to 30

0, 1, 2, 3, 4, 5, 6 . . . 30

Patterns

△ ○ △ ○ △ ○ △ . . .

±

3 + 1 = 4   5 − 1 = 4

Fact families

1 + 3 = 4   4 − 1 = 3
3 + 1 = 4   4 − 3 = 1

Fractions

1   ½ ½

Place value

T	O
3	5	= 35

Money

1¢ 5¢ 10¢ 25¢ $1.00

First Grade

Counting by 1s, 2s, 5s, 10s to 100

1, 2, 3, 4, 5, 6, 7 . . . 100
2, 4, 6, 8, 10, 12 . . . 100
5, 10, 15, 20, 25 . . . 100
10, 20, 30, 40 . . . 100

Patterns

△ ○ ▭   △ ○ ▭   △ ○ ▭ . . .

±

11 + 3 = 14   64   38   3
14 − 6 = 8   +23   −12   5
                   87   26   +2
                                      10

Fact Families

4 + 3 = 7   7 − 4 = 3
3 + 4 = 7   7 − 3 = 4

Comparison

7 > 3   16 < 23   25 = 25

Place value

H	T	O
3	4	7	= 347

Fractions

1   ½   ⅓   ¼   ⅛

Money

1¢ 5¢ 10¢ 25¢ 50¢

10¢ 1¢ 1¢ = 5¢ 5¢ 1¢ 1¢

Second Grade

Counting by 1s, 2s, 5s, 10s to 1,000

1, 2, 3, 4, 5, 6 . . . 1,000
2, 4, 6, 8, 10 . . . 1,000
5, 10, 15, 20, 25 . . . 1,000
10, 20, 30, 40, 50 . . . 1,000

±

$8 + 7 = 15$ $19 - 4 = 15$

Regrouping

$$\begin{array}{r} \overset{1}{2}3 \\ +\ 7 \\ \hline 30 \end{array} \qquad \begin{array}{r} \overset{1}{2}\overset{1}{3} \\ -\ 7 \\ \hline 16 \end{array}$$

Fact families

$12 + 3 = 15$ $15 - 3 = 12$
$3 + 12 = 15$ $15 - 12 = 3$

Comparison

$352 > 248$ $672 = 672$
$173 < 183$

Fractions

1   1/2   1/3   1/4   1/8

Place value

Th	H	T	O
3	4	2	7

= 3,427

Money

1¢ 5¢ 10¢ 25¢ 50¢ $1, $5 $10 $20

$$\begin{array}{r} \$\ 5.42 \\ +\ \$\ 3.27 \\ \hline \$\ 8.69 \end{array}$$

Third Grade

Counting to 10,000

1, 2, 3, 4, 5, 6 . . . 10,000

Place value

TTh	Th	H	T	O
3	1	2	6	5

= 31,265
Thirty-one thousand two hundred and sixty-five

Expanded form

$30,000 + 1,000 + 200 + 60 + 5 = 31,265$

Decimals

32.7
(tenths)

Rounding

$9,986 \sim 10,000$

+/−/×/÷

$37 + 29 = 66$ $41 \times 3 = 123$
$264 - 77 = 187$ $9\overline{)81}$

$$\begin{array}{r} 16\ \text{R1} \\ 2\overline{)33} \\ -2 \\ \hline 13 \\ -2 \\ \hline 1 \end{array}$$

Multiplication

$6 \times 7 = 42$
$6 \times 8 = 48$
$6 \times 9 = 54$

Fact families

$6 \times 9 = 54$ $54 \div 9 = 6$
$9 \times 6 = 54$ $54 \div 6 = 9$

Fractions

1   1/2   1/3   1/4   1/8
2/4 = 1/2   1/4 + 2/4 = 3/4
1/2 = .5

Money

1¢ 5¢ 10¢ 25¢ 50¢ $1, $5, $10, $20

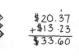

$$\begin{array}{r} \$20.37 \\ +\ \$13.23 \\ \hline \$33.60 \end{array}$$

Fourth Grade

Numbers 1 to 100,000	1, 2, 3, 4, 5, 6 ... 100,000
Standard form	HTh 8 | TTh 9 | Th 3 | H 2 | T 1 | O 7 = 893,217
Expanded form	800,000 + 90,000 + 3,000 + 200 + 10 + 7
Word form	eight hundred ninety-three thousand two hundred and seventeen
Place value	8.73 (tenths / hundredths)
Decimals	
Rounding	7,789 ~ 8,000
Negative numbers	-4 -3 -2 -1 0 1 2 3 4
Prime numbers	1, 3, 5, 7, 11, 13 ...
+/−/×/÷	637 × 24 6)426 41 R1 6)247
Multiplication facts to 10	4 × 4 = 16 4 × 5 = 20 4 × 6 = 24
Fact families	2 × 8 = 16 16 ÷ 2 = 8 8 × 2 = 16 16 ÷ 8 = 2
Fractions	6/12 = 1/2 6/8 = 3/4 = .75 9/4 = 2 1/4 = 2.25
Money	$ 1.34 + $ .95 $2.76 − $2.17

Fifth Grade

Numbers 1 to 1,000,000	1, 2, 3, 4, 5, 6, 7 ... 1,000,000
Place value	M 2 | HTh 3 | TTh 6 | Th 1 | H 4 | T 1 | O 5 = 2,361,415
Standard form	
Expanded form	2,000,000 + 300,000 + 60,000 + 1,000 + 400 + 10 + 5
Word form	two million three hundred sixty-one thousand four hundred and fifteen
Decimals	9.325 (tenths, hundredths, thousandths)
Rounding	6,889 ~ 7,000
Percentage	75% = 3/4 = .75
± Integers	-5 -4 -3 -2 -1 0 1 2 3 4 5 -4 + 2 = -2 -3 × -4 = -12 -5 × 3 = -15
Mixed numbers	16/3 = 5 1/3
Prime factors	48 12 4 3 4 2 2 2 2
Exponents	$2^4 × 3$ (2 × 2 × 2 × 2) × 3
+/−/×/÷	734 × 227 32)692
Fractions	14/20 = 7/10 4/6 + 2/6 = 6/6 = 1 1/2 × 1/2 = 1/4 3/4 ÷ 1/4 = 3
Money	$3.61 × .85 $1.50)3.50

Algebra

Kindergarten

Sorting, classifying, identifying

First Grade

Number sense

$+/-/=$

Word problems

$+/-/=$

$$3 + \_ = 7 \qquad 8 - \_ = 5$$

$$4 - 1 = 3$$

Second Grade

Communicative and associative rules

Number sentence with symbols

$+/-/=$

Problems using data from charts and graphs $\pm$

$$3 + 2 = 5 \quad \text{so} \quad 2 + 3 = 5$$

$$3 + 2 = 5$$

$$5 - 3 = 2 \text{ more } \text{Ö} \text{ than } \text{Ɛ3}$$

Third Grade

Numeric equations and inequalities
Communicative and associative properties
Unit conversions
Operational symbols
Functional relationships and patterns

$$3 + n = 7$$
$$2 + n > 1$$
$$2 \times 3 = 6 \quad so \quad 3 \times 2 = 6$$

12 inches = 1 foot

$$4 \_ 3 = 12$$

4 legs   so   (4) $4 \times 4 = 16$ legs

Fourth Grade

Operational symbols
( ) in math expressions
Formulas
Properties of equality

$$n \times 3 = 12$$
$$25 \div \square = 5$$
$$3 \_ 6 = 18$$

$$4 + (2 \times 3) =$$
$$4 + 6 = 10$$

$$y = 4x + 2$$
$$x = 2$$
$$y = 4(2) + 2$$
$$y = 10$$

$$A = lw$$

$$2(6 + 2) = (8) \times 2$$
$$8 + (2 + 3) = 5 + 8$$

Fifth Grade

Identifying and graphing ordered pairs
Using graphs or equation data to solve problem situations
Using letters to represent unknown numbers
Distributive properties

$$\square - \diamond = \_ more \square$$
$$5 - 2 = 3 \, more \square$$

(-2, 2)   . (2, 2)
(-2, -2) .   . (2, -2)   (x, y)

$$y = 3x + 5 \qquad x = 2$$
$$= 3(2) + 5$$
$$= 6 + 5$$
$$= 11$$

$$3 + (6 \times 4) =$$
$$6 + (3 \times 4) =$$

Measurement and Geometry

Kindergarten

Time

Units of measure

Calendar: days of the week, months of
the year

Geometric shapes

Planes and solid objects

First Grade

Length (in./cm), weight, and volume

Time: hour, half hour

Identifying and classifying

Planes and solid objects

Proximity and position

Second Grade

Length (in./cm), weight, and volume
Units of measure: in./cm
Time: hour, half hour, quarter hour
Identifying, classifying, and describing
Planes and solid objects
Time equivalents
Duration of time intervals

August = 31 days
1 year = 365 days
11 a.m. – 6 p.m. = 7 hours

Third Grade

Length, volume, and mass
Area and volume of a solid
Perimeter
Attributes of triangles
Quadrilaterals
Polygons
Right angles and angles
Identifying, classifying, and describing
Planes and solid objects

Fourth Grade

Area and volume of a solid

Perimeter

2-D coordinate grids

Parallel and perpendicular lines

Radius and diameter of a circle

Congruent and similar figures

Symmetry

Right, obtuse, and acute angles

Attributes of triangles

Identifying, classifying, and describing

Planes and solid objects

Quadrilaterals

Fifth Grade

Area and perimeter formulas

Sum of angles in a triangle

2-D coordinate grids

Parallel and perpendicular lines

Radius and diameter of a circle

Congruent and similar figures

Right, obtuse, and acute angles

Geometric solids

Defining triangles and quadrilaterals

Constructing 2-D patterns

Volume

2-D vs. 3-D objects

Measuring, identifying, and drawing
  angles: protractor and compass

Statistics, Data Analysis, and Probability

Kindergarten

Sorting by common attributes

Data collection

Recording with pictograph

Simple patterns

First Grade

Sorting objects, data by common attributes

Bar graph and pictograph

Tally charts

Simple repeating patterns

Second Grade

Recording number data

Graphs and charts

Mode and range

Extended patterns

Tally charts

range = 6 - 10   (10 - 6 = 4)
mode = 9

3, 6, 9, ☐, ☐, ☐

© The McGraw-Hill Companies, Inc.

Third Grade

Certain, likely, unlikely, improbable

Outcomes and probability

Bar graph

Line plots, coordinate points

Predicting future events

Mean, mode, and range

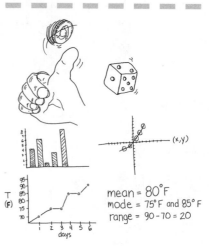

mean = 80°F
mode = 75°F and 85°F
range = 90 - 70 = 20

Fourth Grade

Formulating survey questions for
   data collection

Graphs, tables, and charts

Mode, median, and range

Representing outcomes

Tables, grids, and tree diagrams

Outcomes and probability

How many pets do you own? What kinds?

(3, 4, 3, 5, 7 3, 6)   mode = 3
median = 5
range = 7 - 3 = 4 (3 to 7)

2 out of 3 = 2/3

Fifth Grade

Mean, median, and mode

Organizing and displaying data

Pie graphs

Bar graphs

Histographs

Line graphs

Comparing data sets

   Fractions and percents

     Identifying and writing ordered pairs

(3, 4, 3, 3, 5, 3, 6, 7, 7, 9) mode = 3
median = 6
mean = 5
range = 9 - 3 = 6

□ = 70%
▦ = 8%
▨ = 15%
▥ = 7%

6/10 = 3/5 = 60% heads so 40% tails
8/10 = 4/5 = 80% heads so 20% tails

(2,3) (3,8) (4,1)

Mathematical Reasoning

Kindergarten

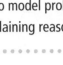

Using tools, strategies, and manipulatives
   to model problems

Explaining reasoning

First Grade

Using tools, strategies, and manipulatives
   to model problems

Determining approach

Explaining reasoning

Making exact calculations

Making connections between

Second Grade

Using tools, strategies, and manipulatives
   to model problems

Defending reasoning

Third Grade

Breaking problems down to simpler parts

Estimating

Explaining reasoning

Supporting solutions with evidence

Making exact calculations

Developing generalizations

Fourth Grade

Sequencing and prioritizing information

How and when to break down a problem

Variety of methodologies

Expressing solutions clearly and logically
   (math notation)

Exact and proximate solutions

Making exact calculations

Developing generalizations

Fifth Grade

Sequencing and prioritizing information

How and when to break down a problem

Variety of methodologies

Expressing solutions clearly and logically
   (math notation)

Exact and proximate solutions

Making exact calculations

Developing generalizations

111

Social Science Overview

Social Science is the study of our world and its people and their interactions. It brings together connections and relationships that give students an understanding of their place and role in their school, community, state, and country as well as in the world. As with any subject area, strands are introduced at the various grade levels and then continued in subsequent grades. They are introduced at age-appropriate levels of understanding. Always follow your curriculum or standards first to ensure that your students have an understanding of the skills they need to prepare them for subsequent learning. You are sometimes laying a foundation and at other times you are building on a foundation that hopefully is already in place. Once that commitment is fulfilled and if time permits, you can branch out into areas of personal interest. The following is an overview of the various strands that may be covered in your district's curriculum and/or state standards.

Careers

Present vs. Past

National Symbols, Icons, and Traditions

Time Lines

Commerce

Conflict Resolution and Communication

Cultural Diversity

Traditional Holidays

State History (generally fourth grade)

United States History (generally fifth grade)

Ancient History (generally sixth grade)

Folklore

Heroes

Economics

Maps and the Globe

Character

Citizenship

Government

Community

Science Overview

Science is divided into three major strands of instruction. Each grade level generally touches on some aspect of instruction in each of the three strands. In turn, each grade level lays a foundation for subsequent learning. The depth of study is geared toward age-appropriate understanding. While certain areas of science instruction may appeal to you, your primary goal should be to teach what is laid out in your standards. This ensures a student's preparedness for the next layer to be added at its designated subsequent grade level. For example, simple machines may be introduced in first grade and then studied in more depth or continued in fifth grade.

Physical Science

Physical science is the study of physical phenomena that exist in nature. The following is a general list of Physical Science substrands that may be covered at your grade level or by grade-level standards.

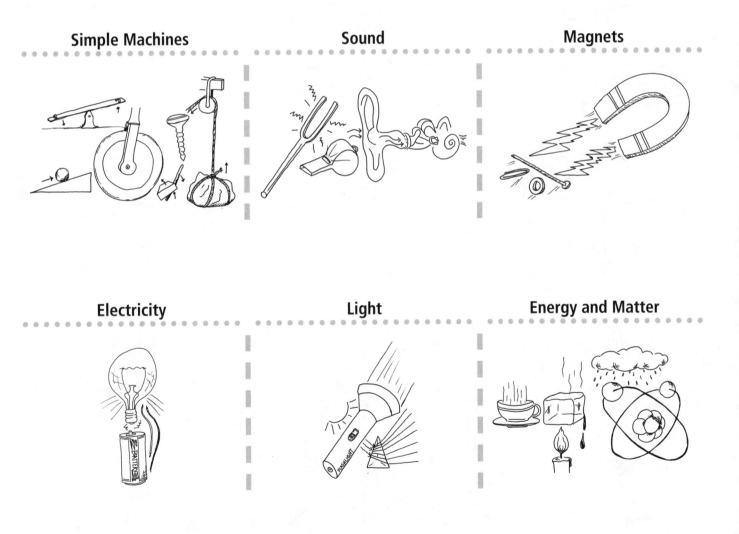

Simple Machines

Sound

Magnets

Electricity

Light

Energy and Matter

Life Science

Life Science is the study of everything pertaining to life. The following is a general list of Life Science substrands. Check your grade-level standards for specificity.

Birds

Mammals

Reptiles

Amphibians

Dinosaurs

Insects and Spiders

Fish

Carnivores

Herbivores

Five Senses

Human Body

Plants

leaf

stem

seed

root

Ocean Life

Food Chain

Earth Science

Earth Science focuses on the Earth and its physical structures, cycles, and relationships. Space Science can fall under this strand as it relates to Earth as a planet. The following is a general list of Earth Science substrands that may be covered at your grade level or by grade-level standards.

Land Forms

Air

Geology (rocks)

Weather and Clouds

Sun and Moon

Seasons

Solar System and Planets

Recycling

Habitats

Endangered Species

Water and Water Cycle

117

Art Overview

A rt is a vital part of a child's education and personal creative expression. Many teachers think that if they can't draw then they can't teach art. Don't fall into this trap. You just need to provide the necessary environment, enthusiasm, materials, and motivation; your students will take care of the rest. The following is a brief summary of the elements of art and the principles of design. With an understanding of these concepts and the basic art materials found in the classroom, anyone can teach art. There are always those teachers who are very creative and artistic and do wonderful projects. Ask for ideas or help or team teach and take on a subject area you are more comfortable with. Still, give it a try. Your students are quite capable and you'll be surprised by the results. Have fun with it.

Elements of Art

Color

Primary: red, blue, yellow
Secondary: orange, violet, green
Value = light or dark
Intensity = bright or dull

Line

Continued stroke
Types:

Straight		Zigzag	
Diagonal		Jagged	
Horizontal		Curvy	
Vertical		Curly	
Thick		Circular	
Thin		Wavy	

Form

Mass of an object (3-D)

Shape

2-D geometric

Texture

Quality of a surface

Rough

Smooth

Space

Area around an object

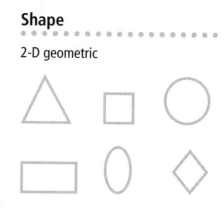

Positive

Negative

Principles of Design

Balance
Asymmetrical

Balance
Radial

Balance
Symmetrical

Theme
Common idea

Repetition
Repeating elements

Movement
How your eye travels
through an art piece

Contrast
Opposing aspects

Dominance
More emphasis on one part

Unity
Fitting together as one

Rhythm
Repeating flow of line or shape

Emphasis
Prominence

Basic Classroom Art Supplies

The following is a basic set of supplies that can be used in the classroom. Not all schools will have all supplies. Check to see what is available and permissible at your school.

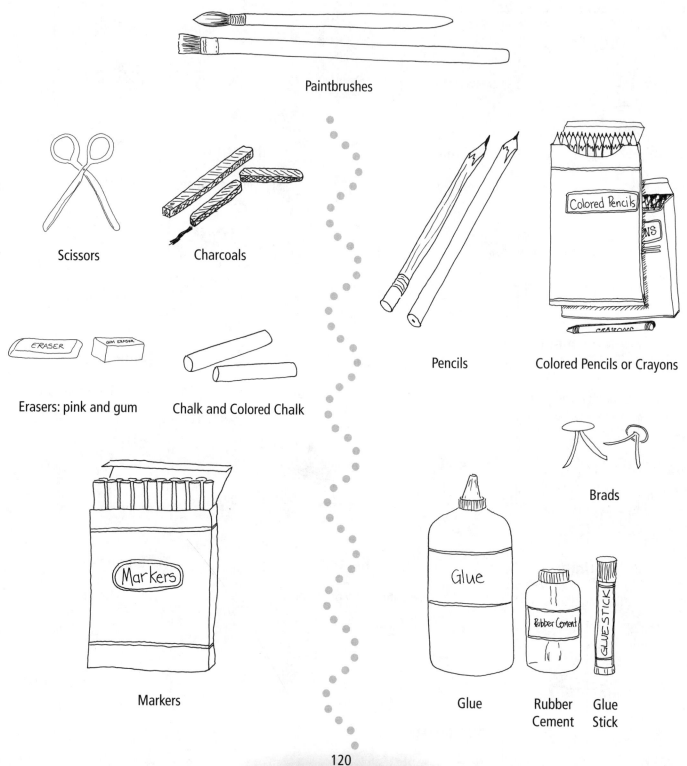

Paintbrushes

Scissors

Charcoals

Pencils

Colored Pencils or Crayons

Erasers: pink and gum

Chalk and Colored Chalk

Brads

Markers

Glue

Rubber Cement

Glue Stick

Oil Pastels

Pastels

Paper: drawing and construction

Tissue Paper

Tape: masking, clear,
book-binding

Tempera Paint

Cord or Yarn

Pipe Cleaners

Watercolor Paints

Color Wheel

One of the fundamental aspects of art is color. Students learn as early as kindergarten how to mix colors to create new ones. There are three primary colors, three secondary colors, and five intermediate colors. There are cool colors and warm colors. Colors that complement each other are complementary colors. One of the best ways to teach color is with a color wheel. The following page has a basic template for creating a color wheel. Here is a basic breakdown of color and suggestions for creating a color wheel.

Can be done with:

Crayons

Colored pencils

Pastels*

Paint*

*Heavier paper (paper plates work well, too)

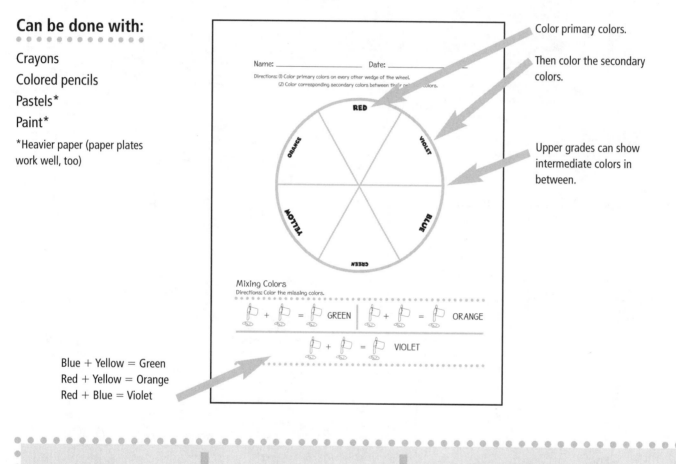

Color primary colors.

Then color the secondary colors.

Upper grades can show intermediate colors in between.

Blue + Yellow = Green
Red + Yellow = Orange
Red + Blue = Violet

Primary Colors

Red

Blue

Yellow

Secondary Colors

Violet

Orange

Green

Cool Colors

Blue

Violet

Green

Warm Colors

Red

Orange

Yellow

Intermediate Colors

Red-violet, Red-orange

Blue-violet, Blue-green

Yellow-orange, Yellow-green

Complementary Colors

(opposite sides of the color wheel)

Red—Green

Blue—Orange

Yellow—Violet

Name: Date:

Directions: (1) Color primary colors on every other wedge of the wheel.
　　　　　　(2) Color corresponding secondary colors between their primary colors.

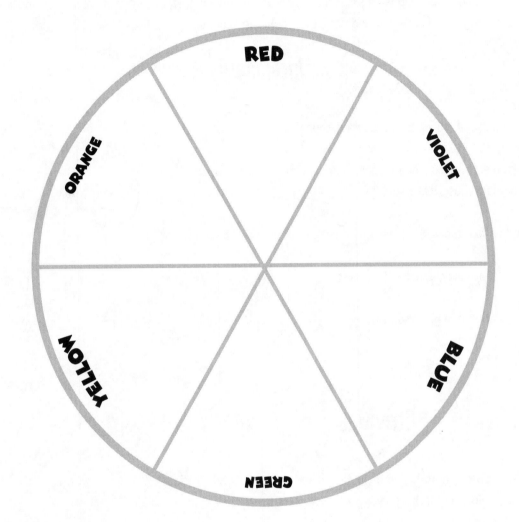

Mixing Colors
Directions: Color the missing colors.

+ = GREEN | + = ORANGE

+ = VIOLET

Music Overview

Music, like visual art, is an excellent creative outlet for students. Many teachers shy away from teaching music, but it doesn't have to be complicated. Again, look to the teachers who have strengths in this area for ideas and advice. Teaming is an excellent option. The following is an overview of some basic music terminology, some suggested activities, and basic classroom instruments.

Vocabulary

Beat: the pulse of music; can be clapped, tapped, etc.

Rhythm: the flow of the music, its movement with various sounds and rests; gives music its personality

Melody: unified tones or pitches that create a tune, have a rhythm

Pitch: high and low characteristic of a sound

Echo: repetition of a given sound

Rest: silent pause in music

Activities

Chart and Sing: Chart the words to a song and sing song while tracking words; very helpful in teaching a song. Also excellent for primary students to build print awareness and left-to-right tracking.

Play Along to a Song: Pass out some classroom instruments and allow students to play along to the beat or melody of a song. Try clapping to the song as a whole class first, then use instruments to play along to the song. Very simple, yet students love it. Try only a few instruments and rotate the instruments.

Pass the Beat: Sit in a circle or at desks. One person claps out a beat, then the entire class echoes the same beat. Each student takes a turn. Can add in actions, too. Try it with an instrument—students echo with clapping and the instrument is passed along to each student for his or her turn.

Basic Classroom Instruments

Classrooms are sometimes equipped with a basic set of instruments that can be used for music instruction. Check with your school and/or other teachers to see if any sets are available to be checked out or borrowed. If none are available, some of the basic ones can be made (see suggestions below). Always establish rules for using instruments to facilitate ease of instruction and maintain order. Oftentimes, especially with the primary grades, some free exploration time (five minutes) with the instruments helps take the edge off when students can get some play out of their system.

Suggested Rules:

1. Do not touch instrument until instructed to do so.
2. Only play instrument when instructed to do so.
3. Listen to and follow directions.
4. Pass instrument to next student when your turn is finished.

Not following the rules will result in you losing your turn with the instrument until the next rotation.

Maraca

Guiro Tone Block

Jingle Clog

Jingle Bells

Hand Castanet

Rhythm Sticks

Sand Blocks

Guiro

Claves

125

Cowbell

Tambourine

Triangle

Cymbals

Bongos

Wood Block

Hand Tom-Tom

Finger Cymbals

Slit Drum

Hand Drum

Do-It-Yourself Instruments

Soda-Bottle Shaker

- Use a plastic soda bottle.
- Fill with beans or rice.
- Cover or decorate with paper.

Kazoo

- Use a toilet paper roll.
- Put wax paper over one end.
- Secure with rubber band.
- Poke hole just below rubber band.
- Hum on open end.

Paper-Plate Shaker

- Decorate and tape two paper plates together.
- Fill with beans or rice.

Rhythm Sticks

Sand Blocks

- Use two wood blocks and sandpaper.
- Cut sandpaper to wrap around three sides of blocks.
- Glue sides and attach.
- Staple to reinforce.

Bucket Drum

Paper-Roll Shaker

- Secure wax paper at each end.
- Fill with rice or beans.

Finger Cymbals

- Use small jar lids.
- Secure elastic strap through a hole.

Mallet

- Attach a cork to a pencil.

Coffee-Can Drum

- Empty a can and remove both ends.
- Cover one end with wax paper, vinyl, or leather.
- Secure with heavy rubber band.

127

Physical Education and Games

Physical education is an important part of a child's education and well-being. It can clear the mind and refresh the body. Often it is hard to find the time to squeeze it in to your schedule with all the other mandated curricular areas. The following are some suggested activities/games that you can use with your students depending on your school policies. Always consult your standards (for skills and required minutes) and select games that support your students' level. Ask other teachers how they fit physical education into their daily/weekly schedule and what activities they use. Most schools provide equipment and have designated play areas. Physical education is an excellent break from the classroom and can build great peer-to-peer relationships as well as teacher-to-student relationships. It can also provide another venue for students to succeed in and build self-confidence. Try it and have fun!

Games can be played collectively as a whole class, in smaller groups, or individually. There are also many games that can be played indoors on inclement weather days.

The following are lists of some suggested games that can give you some options to start with.

Small Group Outdoor Games

Four Square
Hopscotch
Handball
Tetherball
Jump rope

Whole Class Outdoor Games

Cat and Mouse
Steal the Bacon
Red Light, Green Light
Duck, Duck, Goose

Indoor Games

Hunter and Prey
Seven-Up
Sparkle
Around the World
Learning Relay

Outdoor Games

(Small Group)

Four Square

King

Description: small-group game

Skills: bounce-serving a ball, bounce-returning a ball

Rules:

1. The game is played on a large square that is divided into four equal smaller squares. A standard soft red rubber 8½-inch kickball is used.

2. Four players each take a square with one being designated the "king" (the #4 square) and the others are numbered off 1–3 around the square. The object is to advance to king (square #4) and stay there.

3. The king serves the ball with one bounce in his or her square and then hits it (with one or two hands) into one of the other three squares.

4. The receiving player hits the ball into any of the other squares after one bounce in their square.

5. Play continues until one player is "out." A player is out when:

   - A serve is unsuccessful (i.e., doesn't bounce into other square)
   - The player hits or is hit by the ball prior to its bouncing in his or her square
   - The ball bounces twice (or is not hit)
   - The ball is hit with a fist
   - The player hits the ball out of bounds (not bouncing in a square)
   - The player momentarily holds the ball
   - The ball bounces over the player's head (the "hitter" is out)

6. The "out" player proceeds to the end of the line and a new player enters the game at the lowest square with the other players rotating to fill in the vacant square.

Hopscotch

Description: skill and coordination game

Skills: hopping, balancing, tossing accuracy

Rules:

1. Played on a hopscotch grid.

2. Each player has a small object that can be tossed to land on grid (beanbag, rock, etc.).

3. Players hop down and back on the grid to start the game. (Single squares are landed in with one foot, doubles with two)

4. Players who successfully complete their trip then take turns tossing objects onto each numbered square (starting with #1), one at a time. They then hop down the grid, always skipping over the square with the object in it. When players reach the #9 square, they turn on one foot and hop back down the grid while pausing to retrieve object.

5. Players must always:

   - Only toss object into consecutive square without it touching any lines
   - Land themselves only in the squares without touching a line, lowering a raised foot, or switching raised foot

Handball

Description: two players bouncing a ball against a wall

Skills: bouncing and hitting a ball, returning a ball

Rules:

1. Two players stand between six feet (the service line) and fifteen feet from the wall.
2. One player serves the ball by hitting it in a bounce to bounce on the ground inside the service area and up to the wall. The ball must then bounce from the wall to the serving area to be counted (must land between six and fifteen feet). Two attempts can be taken.
3. Player 2 then hits the ball on the bounce to the ground and up to the wall. It cannot bounce twice.
4. Play now continues with each player taking turns. At this point, the ball can hit anywhere in the court and even be hit on the fly.
5. Play continues until:
   - A good serve is not made in two tries
   - The serve doesn't rebound into service area or is hit on the fly
   - The ball is hit after bouncing twice
   - A player interferes with (fouls) another player
   - A ball bounces out of the court
6. Then a new player rotates in and the existing player serves.

15 ft. Serving line

6 ft. Serving line

Serving area

Baseline

Tetherball

Description: two players serving and hitting a ball attached to a pole

Skills: serving and hitting a moving ball

Rules:

1. Two players play on a tetherball court.
2. One player serves, the other player gets to (1) dictate the direction of the serve and (2) choose his or her side of the court.
3. The server tries to hit the ball around the pole again and again to wind it around the pole.
4. Ball is officially in play when the receiver hits it and then tries to unwind the rope by hitting the ball in the opposite direction and wind it back around in this opposite direction.
5. The player who completely winds the rope and ball around the pole is the winner.
6. Play is stopped if and forfeited if:
   - A player hits the ball with anything other than his or her hand.
   - The ball or rope is caught or held in play.
   - The pole is touched.
   - A player steps in the neutral zone
   - The ball is completely wrapped around pole on serve and the receiver has not had an opportunity to hit the ball.

Neutral zone

Jump Rope

Jumping rope is an excellent cardiovascular and coordination activity. Most schools have standard equipment. A plastic rope can be purchased, or a rope can be made from a heavy cotton rope. As with any game, supervision is important. Working with students on taking turns and proper conduct is the key to independent success. The following are some jump-rope variations.

Single Jump Rope

- Single rope (shorter)
- One jumper
- Jump or skip, stationary or moving

Single Rope Paired

- Single rope
- Two turners
- One or two jumpers
- Fun with jump-rope rhymes

Double Dutch

- Two ropes simultaneously
- Two turners
- One or two jumpers
- Fun with jump-rope rhymes

Group Jump

- Single rope
- One student in the center of a circle
- Several jumpers in a circle
- Center student spins the rope around the circle.
- Students jump over rope as it passes them.
- Supervision is recommended.

Outdoor Games

(Whole Class)

Cat and Mouse

Description: a circle game with up to twelve players

Skills: running and dodging; tagging

Rules:

1. Students form a circle by joining hands.
2. One student is selected to be the "cat," another to be the "rat."
3. The cat starts outside the circle with the rat inside the circle.
4. The cat tries to catch or tag the rat.
5. Students assist the rat by raising and lowering joined hands so the rat can move in and out of the circle.
6. Students prevent the cat from catching or tagging the rat by lowering and raising their hands, whichever is necessary.
7. Once the rat is caught or tagged, both choose replacements to play again.

Tips:

- Have two cats or rats.
- Have students unclasp hands if game is too slow.
- As with any game, *discuss safety* to avoid unnecessary accidents.

Steal the Bacon

Description: yard game with two teams of about eight players

Skills: running and dodging

Rules:

1. Two teams each number off and line up facing each other with same numbers at opposite ends (diagonal).
2. A bean bag, knotted rag, or stuffed animal—the "bacon"—is placed in the center.
3. Teacher calls a number and both players with the called number race to the center to retrieve the bacon and return it to their side without being tagged by the other player.
4. Players can run anywhere between the lines to avoid being tagged.
5. Once a player crosses the line or is tagged, the bacon is returned and both players return to their respective positions.

Tips:

- Players who steal the bacon without being tagged score 2 points.
- Players who successfully tag a player with the bacon score 1 point.
- Call two numbers at once (four players = two teams).
- As with any game, *discuss safety* to avoid unnecessary accidents.

Red Light, Green Light

Description: tag game

Skills: running and stopping on signal

Rules:

1. One student is chosen as "it" and the class lines up along a line facing the student, whose back is turned to the class (twenty-five to thirty feet apart).

2. Selected student calls "green light" to start class running toward him or her.

3. Selected student calls "red light" to stop students and turns to catch any students that are moving (have not stopped).

4. Any students caught moving must return to the start line. The remaining students continue to play from their newly advanced position until one player makes it to the finish line.

5. The first player to reach the finish is then designated "it."

Tips:

- Increase or decrease the distance students travel.
- As with any game, *discuss safety* to avoid unnecessary accidents.
- Have students connect to honesty by being able to admit when they moved after the call to stop.

Duck, Duck, Goose

Description: running game, two at a time

Skills: listening, running around a circle, passing to the right

Rules:

1. Class sits in a circle, and one student is designated "it."

2. "It" student walks around outside of circle tapping each student and calling "duck."

3. "It" student taps a student and calls "goose" to stand and race him or her around the circle in the opposite direction back to the vacated spot.

4. The first student to reach the spot sits and the remaining student proceeds around the circle tapping students and calling "duck" until he or she selects the next goose.

Tip:

- As with any game, *discuss safety* to avoid unnecessary accidents.

Indoor Games

Hunter and Prey

Description: indoor game with two players

Skills: balance and coordination

Rules:

1. A designated traffic pattern around the room is established.
2. Two players are chosen to be "hunter" and "prey" and are placed at opposite ends of the classroom.
3. Each player balances an eraser or beanbag on his or her head and cannot touch it.
4. Both players start to walk, and the hunter must tag the prey without losing the balanced object from his or her head.
5. If the prey is tagged or loses the object, he or she chooses a new prey.
6. This new prey then chases the hunter.
7. Whoever is tagged and/or loses the object chooses a replacement and the chase is switched.

Tips:

- Make sure the traffic pattern is obstacle- and feet-free to avoid tripping.
- As with any game, *discuss safety* to avoid unnecessary accidents.

Seven-Up

Description: tagging and guessing game

Skills: none

Rules:

1. Seven players are chosen to stand in front of the classroom and a group leader is appointed.
2. The group leader calls to the remaining seated students "Heads down!"
3. Students close their eyes, lower their heads, and leave one arm raised.
4. The seven chosen students circulate and each taps one student, who then lowers his or her hand, and the player returns to the front of the room.
5. When all seven players have returned to the front of the class, the leader calls "Heads up, seven-up!"
6. All seated students raise their heads and the seven "tapped" students stand beside their desks.
7. The leader asks each player to guess who tagged them.
8. A correct guess exchanges a student and his or her tapper. If the guess is incorrect, the student remains in his or her seat and the player retains his or her position in the seven.
9. The game continues once all guesses and exchanges have been made.

Tips:

- The leader needs to make sure all seven players have been tapped and their hands are lowered.
- Peekers can be eliminated from the game.
- Incorrect guessers can leave a thumb up so that others can have a turn to be tapped.

Sparkle

Description: spelling game

Skills: spelling and concentration

Rules:

1. Teacher calls out a word to be spelled and selects a student to give the first letter.
2. Student says first letter. Teacher points to another student to give the second letter.
3. Continue until entire word is spelled.
4. If a student misses a letter, he or she sits, and another student is called to give the letter.

Around the World

Description: reading game

Skills: word recognition

Rules:

1. Teacher has a set of words written on flash cards.
2. A student is selected to stand behind another student.
3. A word from the card set is shown to both students, and the first to read it moves behind the next student.
4. The next word is shown, and the first to read it advances.
5. The goal is to make it around the entire classroom (around the world).

Learning Relay

Description: math and spelling game

Skills: computation and spelling

Rules:

1. The class is divided into two teams, evenly broken down and mixed by student ability.
2. A student from each team is selected to start the game. They are called to the board, which has been divided in half.
3. Teacher calls out a math fact to be solved or a word to be spelled.
4. Players race to write and solve the problem or spell the word on their respective side of the board.
5. First player to finish successfully wins a point for his or her team.
6. Both players then select the next player from their team to go. Points are tallied.

Bilingual Overview

It is not uncommon to have students whose primary or first language is not English. These students are often categorized as English Language Learners, or ELL. Depending on the ELL population at your given school, you may or may not have a designated bilingual program or an instructional support plan. The following is a simple overview of an ESL (English as a Second Language) program and instructional strategies. Your school or district should have a specific plan that they follow, along with support curriculum and assessments. Check with your school's administration and other teachers for guidelines and strategies.

Common Acronyms and Terms in a Bilingual Program

ELL: English Language Learner

ESL: English as a Second Language

ELD: English Language Development

SDAIE: Specifically Designed Academic Instruction in English

TPR: Total Physical Response

Comprehensible Input: information delivered on a level that is understandable for a given ELD level

Reminders:

- Be sensitive and create a supportive environment.
- Access prior knowledge and make connections to a student's background, culture, and life experiences (creates meaningful learning).
- Pull the key vocabulary and skills to simplify content.
- Increase level of interaction (class, groups, partners) to promote practice through discussion (creates purposeful learning).
- Allow for plenty of speaking and writing time (multiple opportunities).
- Provide comprehensible input (gear instruction to meet the needs specific to the ELD level).

In your school or district, there may be specific strategies along with an adopted ESL program that can assist you in meeting the needs of your ELL students. Be sensitive to the needs of ELL students—learning a new language is a process, not a barrier. It takes real experiences and opportunities to learn a second language.

SDAIE (Specifically Designed Academic Instruction in English)

- SDAIE is strategic instruction that layers lessons to review vocabulary and concepts according to a student's needs. It can target and narrow a lesson's focus, making it easier for the ELL student (comprehensible input). This is an excellent strategy that shouldn't be limited to just ELL students.
- Helps students gain access to information (specifically at the higher ELD levels [3–5])
- With this strategy, the teacher understands the students' struggles, what they know, and what they need to know.

Realia (part of SDAIE)

- Tangible items that can be used to introduce vocabulary (e.g., plastic fruit, items of clothing, etc.).
- Students can touch, hold, and role-play to create "real" learning experiences.

Preteach/Reteach (part of SDAIE)

- Involves preteaching a lesson's vocabulary or concepts to the ELL students
- Increases familiarity/builds background knowledge
- Involves reteaching the key vocabulary and concepts after the lesson has been taught
- Reviews and reinforces

TPR/Role-Play (part of SDAIE)

- Total physical response involves physically executing described actions.
- "Sit down and open the book" = sitting down and opening a book
- Role-playing involves acting out and practicing real-life scenarios and practicing dialogue situations.
- Real learning experiences

Pictures/Graphic Organizers (part of SDAIE)

- "A picture is worth a thousand words."
- Pictures of individual items or of story scenarios
- Graphic organizers to simplify information

There are five levels of ELD. ELD instruction and its delivery is often geared toward meeting the needs of students at their ELD level. These levels help you, the teacher, understand a student's language capabilities. The goal is to move at least one ELD level per year, eventually redesignating into a "fluent English speaker" status. The following is a very simplified look at each level. If engaged in a lesson, students would communicate by:

ELD 1

- responding nonverbally to using a few words.
- pointing to pictures to respond.
- drawing pictures to communicate.

ELD 2

- giving verbal responses of one to two words.
- using yes/no responses.
- writing phrases with invented spellings.

ELD3

- giving verbal responses in short phrases (omitting words or verbs).
- responding to "whys?"—can elaborate.
- writing phrases to simple sentences (conventional spelling starts).

ELD 4

- conversing verbally with few errors.
- answering in discussion.
- writing related sentences with strong vocabulary and few errors.

ELD 5

- responding verbally like a native speaker.
- having discussions like a native speaker.
- writing with the ease of a native speaker.

Sponge Activities

Sponge activities are an excellent, productive way to make use of down time or those five- to ten-minute gaps in the day before a transition (lunch/recess) or at the end of the day. They challenge students to think in a fresh, "out of the box" way that is fun and purposeful. The following are some suggested sponge activities that can be used.

Primary-Grade Sponges

- Be ready to tell one playground rule.
- Be ready to tell me the names of the students in our class whose names begin with *P* or *M* (etc.).
- Be ready to draw something that is only drawn with circles.
- Be ready to tell a good health habit.
- Have a color on the board. Have students draw something that color.
- Say numbers, days of the week, or months, and have children tell what comes next.
- "I went to the sporting goods store and I bought . . ."—each child names an item.
- What number comes between these two numbers: 31–33, 45–47 (etc.)?
- What number comes before or after 46, 52, 13 (etc.)?
- Have a word written on the board. Students make a list of words that rhyme.
- Have a word written on the board. Students make a list of words that have the same long or short vowel sound.
- Put spelling words in *abc* order.
- Count to 100 by twos, fives, tens, etc.—either orally or in writing.
- Use T-squares to drill math fundamentals.
- Think of animals that live in the jungle, on a farm, in the mountains, in water, etc.
- Give the names of fruits, vegetables, meats, etc.
- Play hangman using the names of students in the class, colors, numbers, etc.
- Play Simon Says.
- Play I Spy.
- List things you can touch, things you can smell, big things, small things, etc.
- List the colors you are wearing.

Primary-Grade Dismissal Sponges

- I Spy—who can find something in the room that starts with *M*, *P* (etc.)?
- Who can find something in the room that has a short **a** sound, a long **o** sound, etc.
- Count in order by twos, fives, tens, etc.
- Say the days of the week, the months of the year, etc.
- What day is it? Month? Date? Year? How many months in a year? Days in a week? Etc.?
- Use flash cards. The first correct response leaves first.
- Review the four basic shapes by having each student point out an object in the room that names the shape it represents.
- Say a word that begins or ends with certain consonants, blends, etc.
- Dismiss by color of eyes, clothes, shoe types, month of birthday, season of birthday, beginning letter of name, etc.
- "What did we learn today?" Student identifies one lesson from the day.

Upper-Grade Sponges

- List the continents of the world.
- Make up three names for rock groups.
- Name as many kinds of natural disasters as you can.
- Take a number. Write it. Now draw a face from it.
- Name as many gems or precious stones as you can.
- Write the names of all the girls or boys in the class.
- Write the names of as many teachers in this school as you can.
- List as many states as you can.
- Write as many as you can: (a) abbreviations; (b) Roman numerals; (c) trademarks; (d) proper names (biographical); (e) proper names (geographical).
- How many countries and capitals can you name?
- How many baseball teams can you name?
- Write down as many cartoon characters as you can.
- List as many kinds of flowers as you can.
- List all the things in your living room.
- Write what you would do if you saw an elephant in your backyard or on your street.
- Name as many kinds of ice cream as you can.

Upper-Grade Sponges (continued)

- List five parts of the body above the neck that have three letters.
- List one manufactured item for each letter of the alphabet.
- List as many nouns in the room as you can.
- List the mountain ranges in the United States.
- Write the twelve months of the year correctly. Stand up when you are done.
- Make a list of five things you can do outside after school.
- List one proper noun for each letter of the alphabet.
- Name as many holidays as you can.
- Write numbers by sixes as high up as you can.
- Name as many balls that are used for sports as you can.
- List as many U.S. presidents as you can.
- List all the work tools you can think of.
- List as many models of cars as you can think of.
- Name all the colors you know.
- How many parts of an auto or computer do you know?
- How many animals that begin with vowels can you list?
- List as many kinds of trees as you can.
- Name as many countries in the world as you can.
- Name as many personal pronouns as you can.
- Name as many kinds of transportation as you can.
- How many different kinds of languages can you name?
- Write as many homonyms as you can (e.g., past, passed).
- You have five children. Make up five names.
- Name as many things that are made of cloth as you can.
- List all the musical instruments you can think of.
- Name as many politicians as you can.
- Name as many wars as you can.
- Name as many types of dogs as you can.
- Scramble ten spelling words. Switch with someone. Unscramble the words.
- List as many things that make people the same as you can.
- List as many things that make people different as you can.
- List as many kinds of soup as you can.
- List all the places you find sand.
- List as many breakfast cereals as you can.

Independent Work Ideas

Independent work is important and gives you a chance to meet with individual students or small groups. Training students to work independently is important to minimize interruptions of instruction. Establishing a consistent routine helps as well as having a set of rules and norms in place. Because students work at different levels and speeds, it is important to provide a routine that meets the needs of a diverse student population. The following is a list of suggested activities and a suggested implementation to assist in the facilitation of independent work time.

Must Do and May Do

- Decide on your Must Dos and May Dos according to your instructional goals.
- Use chart paper or dry erase board.
- Gradually introduce activities until students can work independently on them (especially in primary grades). Practice before you attempt to work with a group—make sure they have it.
- Have templates, copies, and paper ready in a designated location.

Suggested Activities

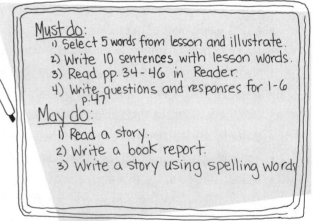

Must do:
1) Select 5 words from lesson and illustrate.
2) Write 10 sentences with lesson words.
3) Read pp. 34-46 in Reader.
4) Write questions and responses for 1-6 p. 47

May do:
1) Read a story.
2) Write a book report.
3) Write a story using spelling words

- Write sentences with designated words.
- Write and illustrate designated words.
- Write a story from a given title using a set of designated words (e.g., using spelling words, try to write a story entitled "My Trip to the Beach").
- Alphabetize a set of words.
- Find rhyming words for a set of designated words.
- Find synonyms or antonyms for words.
- Add prefixes or suffixes to words.
- Look up words in the dictionary.
- Find words or vocabulary and cite an example from a story.
- Read a designated story.
- Write a book report.
- Select an activity from the extra work basket (always run off extra work or assignments and make them available).
- Write questions with *who, what, when, where, why,* and *how* that ask about a story or topic (can also partner trade).
- Write a number as many ways as you can think of (e.g., $9 = 4 + 5$, $13 - 4$, 3×3, etc.).
- Write and illustrate story problems with designated problems or numbers.

RULES
for Independent Work
1. Stay on task.
2. Maintain a quiet work environment.
3. Ask at least 3 other students for help prior to the teacher.
4. Complete "Must do's" before "May do's"

Suggested Rules

- Use indoor voices and keep a quiet environment.
- Stay on task.
- Ask at least three other students for assistance prior to interrupting the teacher with a question.
- Complete Must Dos prior to starting May Dos.

Book Reports

ook reports are an excellent way to reflect and build comprehension. Reports can be used to evaluate your students' comprehension and understanding. Your students can respond to specific questions, write about a character from the book, retell the story, etc. The following are three book-report forms you can use to get started. Choose the report that best meets the needs of your students and supports the standards. As always, check with your school for any school adopted book report forms as well as with other teachers.

Beginning Book Reports

This is the most basic of reports. Kindergarten students can even dictate their book reports and then illustrate them. Here is a list of the key components found in a beginning report:

Name

Date

Title

Author

Illustrator

Three sentences on what the book is about

Student's illustration

Intermediate Book Report

An intermediate book report goes beyond a simple summary and asks for the student's favorite part. Here is a list of the key components found in an intermediate report:

Name

Date

Teacher

Room

Title

Three sentences on what the book is about

Three sentences on student's favorite part

Student's illustration

Advanced Book Report

Here is a list of the key components found in an advanced report:

Name, Date, Teacher, Grade, Room

Title, Author, Illustrator, Copyright, number of pages

Genre

Outline

Student's report

Student's illustration

Book Report

Name: _____

Date: _____

Title: _____

Author: _____

Illustrator: _____

Write three sentences telling what the book is about.

_____

_____

_____

_____

_____

_____

_____

_____

_____

Draw a picture about the story (on the back). Include characters in the setting.

Book Report

Name: _____

Date: _____

Teacher: _____

Room: _____

Title: _____

1. Tell what the book is about (three or more sentences):

_____
_____
_____
_____
_____
_____
_____
_____
_____

2. What was your favorite part (three or more sentences)?

_____
_____
_____
_____
_____
_____
_____
_____
_____

3. Draw a picture about the story (on the back).

BOOK REPORT

Name: _____

Date: _____

Teacher: _____

Grade: _____

Room: _____

BOOK INFORMATION

Title: _____

Author: _____

Illustrator: _____

Copyright date: _____

Number of pages: _____

Genre: ☐ Fiction ☐ Nonfiction ☐ Fable ☐ Fantasy
☐ Fairy Tale ☐ Expository ☐ Biography ☐ Autobiography

BOOK REPORT OUTLINE

Select an outline to assist you in writing your book report.

☐ 1. (a) State subject. (b) List three facts you learned. (c) Describe the most interesting part.

☐ 2. Describe: (a) the main characters (b) the setting (c) the conflict or problem (d) the resolution
(e) a personal connection or opinion.

_____

_____

_____

_____

_____

_____

_____

_____

_____

_____

_____

_____

_____

_____

_____

_____

_____

Draw a picture on the back of your favorite part of the story.

Journals

Journals are an excellent way to reflect on learning across the curriculum. They give students the opportunity to summarize, predict, record, illustrate, and demonstrate what they have learned in a purposeful way. Journals can be easily assembled by stapling the desired journal pages together with a cover sheet (construction paper, student-designed cover, etc.). You may even color-code them for their specific subject (e.g., green for science or red for math). Journals keep an ongoing record of what is being covered in a particular subject. They can be used at conference time to show parents what is being taught and how their child is participating in the process. You may find it easier, especially in the primary grades, to collect them and keep them in a designated location with an appointed journal monitor to distribute them as needed or keep in individual desks for easy access. Journals can be guided or independent. They can make an excellent daily warm-up when set up prior to going home and then recorded in the next morning. The following journals have been included in this book for your use. Be creative—ask others how they use journals in their classrooms. Journals create powerful, meaningful learning.

In the News Journal

Current events

School events

Daily/Weekly lesson summaries

Response Journal

Response to literature

Response to events

Response to lessons

Math Journal

Story problems

Problem explanations

Vocabulary/illustrations

Science Journal

Observations

Predictions

Summaries

Data

Labeled illustrations

Social Science Journal

Historical events

Holidays

Customs

Traditions

Blank Journal

Story writing

Quick writes

Daily journal

In the News Journal

Name: _____ Date: _____ Class: _____ Room: _____

_____

_____   _____
_____   _____
_____   _____
_____   _____
_____   _____
_____   _____
_____   _____
_____
_____   _____
_____   _____
_____   _____
_____   _____
_____   _____
_____   _____
_____   _____
_____

_____   _____
_____   _____
_____   _____
_____   _____
_____   _____
_____   _____
_____   _____
_____   _____
_____   _____
_____   _____

Name: _____ Date: _____

Name: _____ Date: _____

1 2 3 4 5

Name: _____ Date: _____

Name: _____ Date: _____

Name: _____ Date: _____

GINA FOREMAN
3000 MAIL WAY
LOS ANGELES, CA
90007

Name: _____ Date: _____

Name: _____ Date: _____

Name: _____ Date: _____

Bibliography

As most teachers know, the current mandated language arts programs and social studies texts are not enough to teach children all they need to know about history and keep them enthused about reading. With this in mind, it is imperative that teachers maintain a varied classroom library of picture books ranging from informational books, folktales, poetry, realistic fiction, fantasy, biographies, and historical fiction stemming from today's multicultural selections. Such a library will enhance the mandated curriculum and bring it to life. More important, a theme-based library makes the books more accessible and readily available. When a child can see himself or herself in the books being read in class, he or she is more likely to stay engaged, ask critical questions, and gain a deeper understanding of the content. Children learn to enjoy books when books of interest are available to them.

Children's Literature by Theme or Topic

Family

Adoff, A. *Black Is Brown Is Tan.* New York: Harper & Row, 1973. ISBN 0-06-020083-9.

Brown, L. K. *Dinosaurs Divorce: A Guide for Changing Families.* Boston: Little, Brown, 1986. ISBN 0329-02773-5.

Bunting, E. *Jin Woo.* New York: Clarion Books, 2001. ISBN 0-395-93872-4.

Clark, Emma Chichester. *No More Kissing.* New York: Random House, 2001. ISBN 0-385-74619-9.

Curtis, J. L. *Tell Me Again About the Night I Was Born.* New York: Harper, 1996. ISBN 0-06-02528-X.

Greenfield, E. *Grandmama's Joy.* New York: Philomel Books, 1980. ISBN 0-399-21064-4.

Hallinan, P. K. *We're Very Good Friends My Brother and I.* Regensteiner, 1973. ISBN 0-516-03659-9.

Jones, R. *Great Aunt Martha.* New York: Dutton Children's Books, 1995. ISBN 0-525-45257-5.

Dorros, A. *Radio Man: A Story in English and Spanish.* New York: Harper Collins, 1993. ISBN 0-06-021547-X.

Flournoy, V. *The Patchwork Quilt.* New York: Dial Books for Young Readers, 1985. ISBN 0-8037-0098-9.

Miles, M. *Aaron's Door.* Boston: Little, Brown (Canada), 1977. ISBN 0-316-57017-6.

Sharmat, M. W. *Sometimes Mama and Papa Fight.* New York: Harper & Row, 1980. ISBN 0-06-025611-7.

Mem, F. *Wilfrid Gordon McDonald Partridge.* New York: Kane/Miller, 1985. ISBN 0-916291-04-9.

Pellegrini, N. *Families Are Different.* New York: Holiday House, 1991. ISBN 0-8234-0887-6.

Similarities and Differences

Bang, M. *When Sophie Gets Angry—Really, Really Angry. . . .* New York: The Blue Sky Press, 1999. ISBN 0-590-18979-4.

Beaumont, K. *I Like Myself.* Orlando, FL: Harcourt Brace, 2004. ISBN 0-15-202013-6.

Bottner, B. *Two Messy Friends.* New York: Scholastic, Hello Reader! and Cartwheel Books, 1998. ISBN 0-590-63285-X.

Bunting, E. *Smoky Night.* San Diego: Harcourt Brace, 1994. ISBN 0-15-201035-1.

Cheltenham Elementary. *We Are All Alike . . . We Are All Different.* New York: Scholastic, 1991. ISBN 0-590-49173-3.

Cohen, B. *Molly's Pilgrim.* New York: Bantam Doubleday Dell Books for Young Readers, 1983. ISBN 0-440-41057-6.

Coles, S. *Come Home with Us!* Sydney: Child's Play International, 1999. ISBN 0-85953-791-9.

———. *Come and Eat with Us!* Sydney: Child's Play International, 1999. ISBN 0-85953-792-7.

———. *Come and Play with Us!* Sydney: Child's Play International, 1999. ISBN 0-85953-793-5.

———. *Come and Ride with Us!* Sydney: Child's Play International, 1999. ISBN 0-85953-794-3.

De Luise, D. *Charlie the Caterpillar.* New York: Aladdin, 1990. ISBN 0-671-79607-0.

Dorros, A. *This Is My House.* New York: Scholastic, 1992. ISBN 0-590-49444-9.

Fox, M. *Whoever You Are.* Orlando, FL: Harcourt Brace, 1997. ISBN 0-15-200787-3.

Gantos, J., and N. Rubel. *Back to School for Rotten Ralph.* New York: Harper Collins, 1998. ISBN 0-06-027532-4.

Gliori, D. *When I'm Big.* New York: Children's Press, 1992. ISBN 1-56402-241-2.

Henkes, K. *Chrysanthemum.* New York: Greenwillow Books, 1991. ISBN 0-688-09699-9.

Heide, F. and J. Gilliland. *The Day of Ahmed's Secret.* New York: Lothrop, Lee & Shepard Books, 1990. ISBN 0-688-14023-8.

Hoffman, M. *Amazing Grace.* New York: Dial Books for Young Readers, 1991. ISBN 0-8037-1040-2.

Kraus, R. *Leo the Late Bloomer.* New York: Harper Collins, 1971. ISBN 0-87807-042-7.

Lester, H. *Hooway for Wodney Wat.* New York: Houghton Mifflin, 1999. ISBN 0-395-92392-1.

Lester, H. *Tacky the Penguin.* New York: Scholastic, 1988. ISBN 0-590-99451-4.

Lovell, P. *Stand Tall Molly Lou Mellon.* New York: Scholastic, 2001. ISBN 0-439-43452-1.

Madrigal, A. *Erandi's Braids.* New York: G. P. Putnam's Sons, 1999. ISBN 0-399-23212-5.

Max, K. W. *Halala Means Welcome! A Book of Zulu Words.* New York: Hyperion Books for Children, 1998. ISBN 0-7868-0414-9.

Rathman, M. *Ruby the Copycat.* New York: Scholastic, 1991. ISBN 0-590-43748-8.

Reitano, John. *What If the Zebras Lost Their Stripes?* Mahwah, NJ: Paulist Press, 1998. ISBN 0-8091-6649-6.

Rohmer, H. *Uncle Nacho's Hat: El Sombrero del Tío Nacho: A Story in English and Spanish.* San Francisco: Children's Book Press, 1989. ISBN 0-89239-043-3.

Simon, N. *Why Am I Different?* Chicago: Albert Whitman, 1979. ISBN 0-8075-9075-6.

Smith, C., Jr. *I Am America.* New York: Scholastic and Cartwheels Books, 2003. ISBN 0-439-43179-4.

Soto, G. *Chato's Kitchen.* New York: G. P. Putnam's Sons, 1995. ISBN 0-399-22658-3.

Steel, D. *Martha's Best Friend.* New York: Delacorte Press, 1989. ISBN 0-385-29801-3.

Taylor, B. *The Best Sign.* Des Moines, IA: Perfection Learning, 1999. ISBN 0-07891-2900-0.

Wells, R. *Yoko.* New York: Hyperion Books for Children, 1998. ISBN 0-7868-0395-9.

Woodson, J. *The Other Side.* New York: G. P. Putnam's Sons, 2001. ISBN 0-399-23116-1.

Immigration, Migration, Social Justice, and Language

Ancona, G. *Barrio: Jose's Neighborhood.* San Diego: Harcourt Brace, 1998. ISBN 0-15-201049-1.

Aliki, B. *Marianthe's Story: Painted Words and Spoken Memories.* New York: Greenwillow Books, 1998. ISBN 0-688-15662-2.

Bunting, E. *Cheyenne Again.* New York: Clarion Books, 1995. ISBN 0-395-70364-6.

———. *Dreaming of America.* New York: Bridge Water, 2000. ISBN 0-8167-6521-9.

———. *How Many Days to America? A Thanksgiving Story.* New York: Clarion Books, 1988. ISBN 0-395-54777-6.

Freeman, R. *Immigrant Kids.* New York: Puffin Books, 1980. ISBN 0-14-037594-5.

Jiménez, F. *La Mariposa.* Boston: Houghton Mifflin, 1998. ISBN 0-395-81663-7.

Lakin, P. *When a Parent Doesn't Speak English.* New York: The Rosen Publishing Group, 1994. ISBN 0-8239-1691-X.

Lachtman, O. *Pepita Talks Twice: Pepita Habla dos Veces: A Story in English and Spanish.* Houston: Piñata Books, 1995. ISBN 1-55885-077-5.

Lawrence, J. *The Great Migration: An American Story.* New York: Harper Collins, 1993. ISBN 0-374-35114-7.

Leitner, I. *The Big Lie: A True Story.* New York: Scholastic, 1992. ISBN 0-590-45569-9.

Levine, E. *I Hate English.* New York: Scholastic, 1989. ISBN 0-590-42305-3.

Levinson, R. *Watch the Stars Come Out.* New York: Penguin, 1985. ISBN 0-14-055506-4.

Miller, Elizabeth I. *Just Like Home/Como en Mi Tierra.* Chicago: Albert Whitman, 1999. ISBN 0-8075-4068-4.

Nagano, E. *Chopsticks from America.* Chicago: Polychrome, 1994. ISBN 1-879965-11-9.

Namioka, L. *Yang the Youngest and His Terrible Ear.* New York: Yearling, 1994. ISBN 0440409179.

Parker, L. K. *Why Mexican Immigrants Came to America.* New York: The Rosen Publishing Group, 2003. ISBN 0-8239-6459-0.

Pérez, A. *My Diary from Here and There: Mi Diario de Aqui Hasta Allá: A Story in English and Spanish.* New York: Lee and Low Books, 2002. ISBN 1-58430-045-0.

———. (2002). *My Diary from Here to There.* San Francisco: Children's Book Press. ISBN 0-89239-175-8.

Pérez, L. *First Day in Grapes.* New York: Lee and Low Books, 2002. ISBN 1-58430-045-0.

Rael, E. O. *What Zeesie Saw on Delancey Street.* New York: Simon & Schuster, 1996. ISBN 0-689-80549-7.

Recorvits, H. *My Name Is Yoon.* New York: Frances Foster Books, 2003. ISBN 0-374-35114-7.

Say, A. *Grandfather's Journey.* Boston: Houghton Mifflin, 1993. ISBN 0395570352.

———. *Tea with Milk.* Boston: Houghton Mifflin, 1999. ISBN 0395904951.

Surat, M. M. *Angel Child, Dragon Child.* New York: Scholastic, 1983. ISBN 0-590-42271-5.

Williams, S. A. *Working Cotton.* New York: Harcourt Brace, Voyager Books, 1992. ISBN 0-15-299624-9.

Whitman, S. *Immigrant Children.* Minneapolis: Carolrhoda Books, 2000. ISBN 1-57505-395-0.

Customs and Traditions

Bulion, L. *Fatuma's New Cloth.* North Kingstown, RI: Moon Mountain, 2002. ISBN 0-9677929-7-5.

Barasch, L. *The Reluctant Flower Girl.* Hong Kong: Harper Collins, 2001. ISBN 0-06-028810-8.

Chavarria-Chairez, B. *Magda's Tortillas.* Houston: Piñata Books, 2002. ISBN 1-55885-286-7.

———. *Magda's Piñata Magic.* Houston: Piñata Books, 2001. ISBN 1558853200.

Cheng, A. *Grandfather Counts.* New York: Lee and Low Books, 2000. ISBN 1584301589.

Chinn, K. *Sam and the Lucky Money.* New York: Lee and Low Books, 1997. ISBN 1880000539.

Daly, N. *What's Cooking, Jamela?* New York: Farrar, Straus & Giroux, 2001. ISBN 0-374-35602-5.

Fine, E. *Under the Lemon Moon.* New York: Lee and Low Books, 1999. ISBN 1-880000-69-5.

Gray, Nigel. *A Country Far Away.* New York: Orchard Books, 1988. ISBN 0-531-05792-5.

Hru, D. *Joshua's Masai Mask.* New York: Lee and Low Books, 1993. ISBN 1-880000-02-4.

Kleven, E. *Hooray, a Piñata.* New York: Dutton's Children's Books, 1996. ISBN 0-525-456-5-8.

Lachtman, O. *Big Enough: Bastante Grande.* Houston: Piñata Books, 1998. ISBN 1-55885-221-2.

Schotter, R. *Passover Magic.* Boston: Little, Brown, 1995. ISBN 0-316-77468-5.

Soto, G. *The Old Man and his Door.* New York: G. P. Putnam's Sons, 1996. ISBN 0-399-22700-8.

———. *Snapshots from the Wedding.* New York: G. P. Putnam's Sons, 1997. ISBN 0-399-22808-X.

———. *Too Many Tamales.* New York: G. P. Putnam's Sons, 1993. ISBN 0-399-22146-8.

Multicultural Fairy Tales

Anderson, H. C. *The Princess and the Pea.* New York: North South Books, 1984. ISBN 0-03-005738-8.

Climo, S. *The Egyptian Cinderella.* New York: Harper Collins, 1989. ISBN 0-690-04824-6.

———. *The Irish Cinderlad.* New York: Harper Trophy, 1989. ISBN 0-06-024396-1.

———. *The Persian Cinderella.* New York: Harper Collins, 1989. ISBN 0-06-026765-8.

Coburn, J. R. *Angkat: The Cambodian Cinderella.* Auburn, CA: Shen's Books, 1998. ISBN 1-885008-09-0.

De La Paz, M. J. *Abadeha: The Philippine Cinderella.* Fremont, CA: Shen's Books, 1991. ISBN 0-9629255-0-0.

Demi. *The Emperor's New Clothes.* New York: Margaret K. McElderry Books, 2000. ISBN 0-689-83068-8.

De Paola, T. *Adelita: A Mexican Cinderella.* New York: Putman Group Juvenile, 2002. ISBN 0-399-23866-2.

Flor, Ada A. *Yours Truly, Goldilocks.* New York: Aladdin, 1998. ISBN 0-689-81608-1.

Geeslin, C. *How Nanita Learns to Make Flan.* New York: Atheneum Books for Young Readers, 1999. ISBN 0-689-81546-8.

Huck, C. *Princess Furball.* New York: Greenwillow Books, 1989. ISBN 0-688-07838-9.

Johnson, T. *Bigfoot Cinderrrrrella.* New York: Penguin Putnam Books for Young Readers, 1998. ISBN 0-399-23021.

Kimmel, E. *The Four Gallant Sisters.* New York: Henry Holt, 1992. ISBN 0-8050-1901-4.

Kimmel, E. A. *The Three Princes.* New York: Holiday House, 1994. ISBN 0-8234-1115-X.

Louie, Ai-Ling. *Yeh-Shen: A Cinderella Story from China.* New York: Philomel Books, 1982. ISBN 0-399-20900-X.

Lowell, S. *Dusty Locks and the Three Bears.* New York: Henry Holt, 2001. ISBN 0-8050-5862-1.

Martin, R. *The Rough-Faced Girl.* New York: G. P. Putnam's Sons, 1992. ISBN 0-698-11626-7.

Minters, F. *Cinder-elly.* Salinas, CA: Hampton-Brown Books, 1994. ISBN 1-56334-723-7.

———. *Sleeping Beauty.* New York: Penguin Group, 1996. ISBN 0-670-87033-1.

Osborne, M. *Kate and the Beanstalk.* New York: Atheneum Books for Young Readers, 2000. ISBN 0-689-82550-1.

Salinas, B. *The Three Pigs: Los Tres Cerdos: Nacho, Tito, and Miguel.* Houston: Piñata Publications, 1998. ISBN 0-934925-05-4.

San Souci, R. *Cendrillon.* New York: Simon & Schuster Books for Young Readers, 1988. ISBN 0-689-80668-X.

Steptoe, J. *Mufaro's Beautiful Daughters: An African Tale.* New York: Harper Collins Children's Books, 1987. ISBN 0-618-06223-8.

Stewig, W. J. *A Spanish Fairy Tale. Florecita and the Iron Shoes.* New York: Apple Soup Books, 1995. ISBN 0-679-84775-8.

Young, E. *Lon Po Po: A Red-Riding Hood Story from China.* New York: Scholastic, 1989. ISBN 0-590-44069-1.

Gender Roles

Allard, H. *It's So Nice to Have a Wolf Around the House.* New York: Doubleday, 1977. ISBN 0-385-11300-5.

———. *Miss Nelson Has a Field Day.* Boston: Houghton Mifflin, 1985. ISBN 0-395-36690-9.

Beck, M. *The Wedding of Brown Bear and White Bear.* Boston: Little, Brown, 1989. ISBN 0-3160-8652-5.

Berry, C. *Mama Went Walking.* New York: Henry Holt, 1990. ISBN 0-8050-1261-3.

Brown, A. *My Dad.* New York: Farrar, Straus & Giroux, 2000. ISBN 0-374-35101-5.

———. *The Tunnel.* New York: Alfred A. Knopf, 1989. ISBN 0-394-84852-X.

Carlstrom, N. W. *Wild Wild Sunflower Child Anna.* New York: Scholastic, 1987. ISBN 0-590-44346-1.

Corey, S. *You Forgot Your Skirt, Amelia Bloomer.* New York, Scholastic Press, 2000. ISBN 0-439-07919-9.

Hilton, N. *A Proper Little Lady.* New York: Orchard Books, 1989. ISBN 0-531-05860-3.

Hoban, R. *Best Friends from Frances.* New York: Harper & Row, 1969.

Moore, E. *The Day of the Bad Haircut.* New York: Scholastic, ICS, 1996. ISBN 0-590-69770-6.

Munsch, R. N. *The Paper Bag Princess.* New York: Annick Press, 1980. ISBN 0-920236-16-2.

Nolen, J. *In My Momma's Kitchen.* New York: Lee & Shepard Books, 1999. ISBN 0-688-12760-6.

Pfanner, L. *Louise Builds a House.* New York: Orchard Books, 1987. ISBN 0-531-05796-8.

Pinkney, B. *JoJo's Flying Sidekick.* New York: Aladdin Library, 1995. ISBN 0-6898-2192-1.

Zolotow, C. *William's Doll.* New York: Harper Trophy, 1972. ISBN 0-06-443067-7.

Nontraditional Families

Caines, F. *Just Us Women.* New York: Harper Trophy, 1982. ISBN 0-06-020942.

Combs, B. *123: A Family Counting Book.* Ridley Park, PA: Two Lives, 2001. ISBN 0-9674468-0-5.

———. *ABC: A Family Alphabet Book.* Ridley Park, PA: Two Lives, 2001. ISBN 0-9674468-1-3.

DeHam, L. *King & King.* Berkeley, CA: Tricycle Press, 2002. ISBN 1-582460-61-2.

Elwin, R., and M. Pause. *Asha's Mums.* Toronto: Women's Press, 1990. ISBN 0-88961-143-2.

Krakow, K. *The Harvey Milk Story.* Ridley Park, PA: Two Lives, 2002. ISBN 0-9674468-3-X.

Lindenbaum, P. *Else-Marie and her Seven Little Daddies.* New York: Henry Holt, 1991. ISBN 0-8050-1752-6.

Loewen, I. *My Mom Is So Unusual.* Kirkland, WA: Pemmican, 1996. ISBN 0-919143-37-7.

Newman, L. *Felicia's Favorite Story.* Ridley Park, PA: Two Lives, 2002. ISBN 0-9674468-56.

———. *Heather Has Two Mommies.* Boston: Alyson Wonderland, 1990. ISBN 1-5583-180-X.

———. *Saturday Is Pattyday.* Toronto: Women's Press, 1993. ISBN 0-93468-52-9.

Okimoto, J., and E. Aoki. *The White Swan Express: A Story About Adoption.* Dumas, AR: Clarion, 2002. ISBN 0-618-16453-7.

Resier, L. *The Surprise Family.* New York: Greenwillow, 1994. ISBN 0-688-11671-X.

Updike, J. *A Child's Calendar.* New York: Holiday House, 1999. ISBN 0-8234-1445-0.

Vigna, J. *My Two Uncles.* Boston: Albert Whitman, 1995. ISBN 0-8075-5507-X.

Willhoite, M. *Daddy's Roommate.* Boston: Alyson Wonderland, 1990. ISBN 1-55583-118-4.

Classroom Preparedness

Home-Study Folders

Home-study folders are very useful in helping students organize their homework assignments and keep track of any paperwork being sent home for parents. They are a good way to introduce parents to your expectations and also serve as a resource to students. They can be easily assembled using any common inexpensive two-pocket folder and then laminating it (later using an exacto knife to open the folders). You may wish to have students color or write their own name on their folders prior to laminating it, making sure they don't color over the text portions. Introduce the folder and its components prior to sending it home so students are familiar with it and can use it as a resource.

Front

Rubber cement works well and doesn't bubble up.

Back

Inside Pockets

Slice back open after laminating.

MY SHAPES

Triangle

Circle

Rectangle

Oval

Square

Diamond

MY COLORS

Red

Orange

Yellow

Green

Blue

LEFT

White

Black

Purple

RIGHT

I CAN COUNT!

1	2	3	4	5	6	7	8	9	10
one	two	three	four	five	six	seven	eight	nine	ten

Name: _____

Grade: _____ Room: _____ Teacher: _____

HOME STUDY

DO I KNOW WHAT I READ?

WHO?

- Author
- Illustrator
- Main characters

WHAT?

- Story sequence: beginning, middle, end
- Story problem

WHEN?

- Story time: time of day, season

WHERE?

- Story setting: Where did it occur?

HOW?

- Story solution

WHY?

- Opinion of story: Did you like the story? Why? What was your favorite part?

SCHOOL INFORMATION

• • • • • • RUBRIC • • • • • •

4 Perfect score, can't ask for more. Look at me, I am a four!

3 Almost perfect, look at me. Doing great, I am a three.

2 Still much to do makes me a two. But I can do it, I'll show you.

1 I have just begun. With hard work, I'll get it done, but for now I'm just a one.

What's my rubric score: 1, 2, 3, or 4?

• • • MONEY • • •

1¢
Penny

5¢
Nickel

10¢
Dime

25¢
Quarter

Alligator
 Bear
 Cat
 Dog
 Elephant
 Fish
 Goat

 Zebra
 Yarn
 X-ray
 Wagon
 Vacuum
 Umbrella

I CAN READ MY SIGHT WORDS!

all	and	are	an	at	be	but	came
for	from	go	got	had	have	he	her
him	his	if	in	is	it	me	of
on	one	out	said	saw	she	so	that
the	their	there	them	then	they	this	to
up	was	we	went	were	with	you	your

I CAN COUNT!

1	2	3	4	5	6	7	8	9	10
11	12	13	14	15	16	17	18	19	20
21	22	23	24	25	26	27	28	29	30
31	32	33	34	35	36	37	38	39	40
41	42	43	44	45	46	47	48	49	50
51	52	53	54	55	56	57	58	59	60
61	62	63	64	65	66	67	68	69	70
71	72	73	74	75	76	77	78	79	80
81	82	83	84	85	86	87	88	89	90
91	92	93	94	95	96	97	98	99	100

 Horse
 Igloo
 Jet
 Kite
 Lion
 Monkey

 Tent
 Snake
 Robot
 Queen
 Pig
 Octopus
 Nest

Prefixes

anti-: against

de-: opposite of

dis-: not the opposite of

en-: cause to

fore-: before

in-: not/in, into

inter-: among, between

mid-: middle

mis-: wrongful

non-: not

pre-: before

re-: again

sub-: under

un-: not, opposite of

Suffixes

-able/-ible: able to do

-en: made of

-er/-or: person that does

-est: most

-ful: full of

-ish: have likeness to

-less: without

-like: similar to

-ly: characteristic of

-ment: action or process

-ness: a state of being

-ous: full of

-tion/-sion: act or process

-y: characterized by

Part of Speech	Definition	Example	
Noun	A person, place, or thing	**Tom** (person) sat on the **bench** (thing) in the **park** (place).	
Pronoun	Takes the place of a noun	Mary is my friend. **She** is tall. (I, he, she, it, we, you, they)	
		Sam's dog is big. **His** dog is big. (my, his, her, me, its, our, your, their)	
Adjective	Describes a noun	The man sat. The **large**, **old** man sat.	
Verb	An action word	The stallion **runs** fast.	
Adverb	Describes a verb	The tortoise walks **slowly**.	
Preposition	Relates nouns or pronouns to other words	The frog jumped **into** the pond.	
Conjunction	Joins words, phrases, or clauses	Sam read **and** Jan wrote a story.	

Name: _____

Grade: _____ Room: _____ Teacher: _____

Home Study

Comprehension Checklist

Who?
- Author
- Illustrator
- Main characters

What?
- Story sequence: beginning, middle, end
- Story problem

When?
- Story time: time of day, season

Where?
- Story setting: Where did it occur?

Why?
- Opinion of story: Did you like the story? Why? What was your favorite part?

How?
- Story solution

Writer's Checklist

Content
- ☐ I have a topic sentence.
- ☐ I have supporting sentences.
- ☐ I have used descriptive words.
- ☐ I restate the topic in the concluding sentence.

Mechanics
- ☐ I have indented my paragraph. ¶
- ☐ I have checked my spelling. thier = their
- ☐ I have used correct punctuation. . ? !
- ☐ I have subject/verb agreement. "they **are**"

The Writing Process

Prewrite → **Draft** → **Edit Revise** → **Proofread** → **Publish** → **Share/Reflect**

School Information

Fractions

Units of Measure

1 pint = 2 cups · 1 quart = 2 pints · 1 half gallon = 2 quarts · 1 gallon = 4 quarts · 1 liter · 1 cup · 1 tablespoon · 1 teaspoon

Money

1¢ **Penny** heads tails · 5¢ **Nickel** heads tails · 10¢ **Dime** heads tails · 25¢ **Quarter** heads tails

Numerator / Denominator

Triangles

Isosceles Triangle

Scalene Triangle

Right Triangle

Equilateral Triangle

Angles

Right Angle

Acute Angle

Obtuse Angle

Circles

Radius

Diameter

Multiplication Table

×	1	2	3	4	5	6	7	8	9	10	11	12
1	1	2	3	4	5	6	7	8	9	10	11	12
2	2	4	6	8	10	12	14	16	18	20	22	24
3	3	6	9	12	15	18	21	24	27	30	33	36
4	4	8	12	16	20	24	28	32	36	40	44	48
5	5	10	15	20	25	30	35	40	45	50	55	60
6	6	12	18	24	30	36	42	48	54	60	66	72
7	7	14	21	28	35	42	49	56	63	70	77	84
8	8	16	24	32	40	48	56	64	72	80	88	96
9	9	18	27	36	45	54	63	72	81	90	99	108
10	10	20	30	40	50	60	70	80	90	100	110	120
11	11	22	33	44	55	66	77	88	99	110	121	132
12	12	24	36	48	60	72	84	96	108	120	132	144

Geometric Forms

Pyramid   **Cube**   **Rectangular Prism**   **Cone**   **Sphere**   **Cylinder**

Place Value

| | Millions | | | Thousands | | | | | | | | |

136,547,821.942

Hundreds, Tens, Ones (Millions); Hundreds, Tens, Ones (Thousands); Hundreds, Tens, Ones; Tenths, Hundredths, Thousandths

Formulas

$A = \frac{1}{2}bh$

$A = l \times w$ $P =$ add all sides
$P = 2(lw)$

$C = 2\pi r$
$(\pi = 3.14)$

$A = l \times h \times w$

Lines

Line   **Line Segment**   **Ray**   **Intersecting Lines**   **Parallel Lines**

Shapes

Square

Rhombus

Rectangle

Parallelogram

Trapezoid

Quadrilateral

Pentagon

Hexagon

Octagon

Weekly Classroom Focus

The next two pages contain reproducibles you can use to send updates home to your students' parents/guardians. This update will let them know what standards you are focusing on in your classroom. This note should contain focus standards according to your state standards. These should be standards that you would like parents/guardians to be aware of and to focus on at home with their child. This sheet can be a valuable resource in getting the parents/guardians to take ownership and responsibility in their child's learning! This will also make your job in the classroom easier.

Weekly Focus Standards

Here are the standards we are working on in class this week! These are things you can focus on at home with your child in order to help reinforce what we are learning in the classroom. Thanks for your support.

Writing/Language Arts _1.2 Use descriptive words when writing._

Math _2.3 Identify one more than, one less than, 10 more than, and 10 less than a given number._

Science/Social Studies _Students should know solids, liquids and gas._

Art _Your student should be able to recognize and use the different types of line in a drawing._

*If you have any questions, please contact Mr./Mrs./Ms. _Wasley_ at phone# _208.444.1000_

- Check with your administration or go online to find your state's standards.

- This sheet is a valuable resource that can increase parental involvement in their child's education.

- Try to send this weekly or monthly—being consistent will mean success!

- Review these standards and this sheet with your students before you send it home. A powerful teaching tool is letting the students know exactly what they are learning.

- Keep standards clear, concise, and focused. You can edit standards and reword them to be more parent friendly.

WEEKLY FOCUS STANDARDS

Here are the standards we are working on in class this week! These are things you can focus on at home with your child to help reinforce what we are learning in the classroom. Thanks for your support.

WRITING AND LANGUAGE ARTS _____

_____

_____

MATH _____

_____

_____

SCIENCE AND SOCIAL STUDIES _____

_____

_____

ART _____

_____

_____

If you have any questions, please contact Mr./ Mrs./ Ms. _____ at phone number _____ .

MONTHLY FOCUS STANDARDS

Here are the standards we are working on in class this month! These are things you can focus on at home with your child to help reinforce what we are learning in the classroom. Thanks for your support.

WRITING AND LANGUAGE ARTS _____

_____

_____

MATH _____

_____

_____

SCIENCE AND SOCIAL STUDIES _____

_____

_____

ART _____

_____

_____

If you have any questions, please contact Mr. / Mrs. / Ms. _____

_____ at phone number _____.

Daily Schedule

Teacher: _____   Room: _____

School: _____   Year: _____

Time	Subject or Activity

Teacher Signals

Whether you're a brand-new teacher or about to retire, almost all of you in the teaching profession have a few tricks to get your students' attention. Teachers in the upper grades don't need these tricks of the trade as much as primary-grade teachers do—and certainly not as much as those teaching kindergarten! Here are a few signal ideas you may want to add to your repertoire.

1. **Turn off the lights.**
   This is universal and works with any age group. The response is instant.

2. **Clap.**
   This is another simple yet effective signal. Any simple rhythm or single clap, "clap once if you're listening!"

3. **Use a catch phrase.**
   This is more directed to primary-grade teachers, and an easy-to-learn phrase will do. A popular one among kindergarten teachers is "Crisscross applesauce!"

Criss Cross..!

4. **Ring a bell.**
   This one is easy and quick. The bell can work for all age groups and is an instant attention-getter. A whistle can be substituted for the bell.

5. **Give me five.**
   This is a nonverbal hand signal used to get students' attention when you don't want any noise. As you put up each finger of one hand, the following happens; one, stop; two, tell a neighbor to stop; three, look; four, listen; and five, wait for a cue or directions.

6. **Use nonverbal cues.**
   A couple of good nonverbal cues can be a lifesaver. If you are talking to a colleague or you simply don't want to yell, a nonverbal signal is great! One of the most common nonverbal signals is two fingers in the air, which is usually the sign for quiet. Experiment and see what works for you.

7. **Insert your idea here.**
   This is where you get to think of your own creative idea. Be brave and have fun experimenting!

Uses for Teacher Signals

Why use a teacher signal? What is its importance? These simple attention-getters have unlimited uses inside or outside of the classroom. The following are reasons teacher signals are necessary and useful for attention-getting in the classroom!

An Emergency
This is perhaps the best reason for a signal. In an emergency, a signal is needed for instant attention: stop, look, and listen.

Change of Subject
A signal to transition your class between two subjects can be a time-saver. This is a great place to include steps after the signal is given.

During a Directed Lesson
This can be a catch phrase or a simple clap. We've all had classes where when one student answers, the entire rest of the class feels free to add in their answers as well. When your students do this or are not all paying attention, try a quick attention-getter. A great signal is, "Clap once if you're listening!"

Guest in the Room
This is a great situation for a nonverbal signal. It could be a sign for the class to quiet down if you happen to be interrupted by a guest at the door. Usually, you're busy talking to the guest and need a signal that doesn't require you to speak.

Recess or Dismissal
Choose one signal that signifies when it's time to leave the room, be it recess or dismissal. Different signals cue different things; a great signal for this is to simply turn the lights off. It's easy and quiet and elicits an instant response.

Student Risk Factors

No matter where you teach, students come to school with their own sets of issues. This can mean anything happening in a child's life outside of school—some things good and some not so good. As teachers, we have an innate sense of when a student is going through adverse or hard times at home. These adversities show up in a variety of ways within the student. This page is a simple reminder of behaviors a student might exhibit when dealing with adverse happenings. These behaviors can often be a subconscious cry for help from the student. If you are experiencing any of these behaviors with a student, investigate and get information about the student. Before drawing any conclusions, talk with that particular student's previous teachers, check student records, get advice from your administrators, talk with the school psychologist and/or counselor, and possibly meet with the parents/guardians. Because a child exhibits one of the behaviors listed below, it doesn't mean you should push the panic button, it simply means you need to pay a little more attention to that student.

- Excessive Absences
- Low Self-Esteem
- Frequent Change of Residence
- Poor Peer Relationships
- Grade Retention
- Disruptive Behavior
- Inability to Tolerate Structure
- Frequent Health Problems

- Single-Parent Family
- English Language Learner
- Immature, Easily Influenced
- Frequent Suspensions or Expulsions

- Easily Distracted
- Inattentive
- Poor Classroom Behavior
- Doesn't Complete Tasks
- Doesn't Submit Homework
- Alternative Living Situation
- Parent Work Schedule
- Other

Just to Let You Know...

To the parent(s) of: _____

Date: _____ From: _____

Reason for the note:

☐ Exceptional Behavior

☐ Super Listener

☐ Great Attitude

☐ Great Work

☐ Excellent Homework

☐ Incomplete or Missing Homework

☐ Poor Attendance or Tardiness

☐ Not Following Directions

☐ Unacceptable Behavior

☐ Other

Comments _____

_____

_____

Please　☐ Sign and return.

　　　　☐ Contact Mr./Mrs./Ms. _____

☐ Talk with your child.

☐ Arrange for a conference.

A Note Home...

To the parent(s) of: _____

Date: _____ From: _____

Reason for the note:

☐ Exceptional Behavior

☐ Super Listener

☐ Great Attitude

☐ Great Work

☐ Excellent Homework

☐ Incomplete or Missing Homework

☐ Poor Attendance or Tardiness

☐ Not Following Directions

☐ Unacceptable Behavior

☐ Other

Comments _____

_____

_____

Please　☐ Sign and return.

　　　　☐ Contact Mr./Mrs./Ms. _____

☐ Talk with your child.

☐ Arrange for a conference.

Teacher's Aide

As the leader of the classroom, you are not only responsible for your students, you are also responsible for your aide. That is if you're lucky enough to have an aide! Depending on your school, the grade you teach, and funding, you may or may not have an aide. If you are unfamiliar with what a teacher's aide is, this is a person who is hired to assist you in your classroom. If you are lucky enough to have an aide, you might be saying, "What do I do with my teacher's aide?" Whether you have been in the class for two or twenty years, you may have questions on how to use your aide successfully. These are some ideas to get you started.

Helpful Tips

1. Make clear what kind of work and participation you want done by your teacher's aide. Give him or her clear and concise direction on what needs to be done each day. Depending on experience, your aide may be very capable and used to working in a classroom setting; however, aides don't usually hold teaching credentials. Manage their time appropriately!

2. Try not to be too friendly. Not being friendly doesn't mean not being nice. This is just to say that keeping a professional relationship makes things much easier when *you* are running a classroom. (There are exceptions to every rule, and you may become close to your room partner.)

3. Remember, you are the teacher! At the end of the day, the class is your vision and your responsibility, so make sure you're the one in charge. That's not to say you need to be disrespectful or dictatorial, it just means you need to be professional and provide your teacher's aide with kind guidance and your vision.

4. Be good to your teacher's aide. Try to smile and promote how helpful they really are. Like teachers, aides perform much better when they are appreciated! The better you are to your aide, the more excited he or she will be to follow your vision for the class.

Teacher's Aide Activities

ere is a list of productive activities that you can have your aide do within your classroom.

Review with Low-Achieving Students

An aide can be very effective working with low-achieving students on a daily basis. Establish a list of students and review skills to give your aide a clear task. This will give him or her a one-to-one relationship with the students, which will make the job more meaningful for your aide.

Assessments

Your aide can help you keep up with assessments. Whether it's recording the scores or actually giving the assessment, your aide can be a time-saver. The only time you would not want the aide to give an assessment is when you want to get a sense for yourself as to where the students are.

Small-Group Review

You may choose to have your aide pull together a small group of students to review particular skills they need to work on.

Individual Guidance

Even though an aide is not a one-to-one type of tutor, he or she can be helpful in keeping one or two students focused on you during a guided lesson. A great tool is to have your aide sit with the student(s) while you are giving the lesson.

Guide the Entire Class in a Lesson

If you as the teacher want to do individual review with students, then your aide could take the class in a guided lesson while you pull students for individual review. You may want to have your aide take the class in case you need to speak with an individual review for a week or two.

Record Keeping

This is an activity that an aide could accomplish in a last-minute circumstance, possibly helping grade an assessment that is due. The other recommendations, however, are better choices for using an aide's time.

180

Teacher's Aide Worksheet

Student's Name: _____   Grade: _____

Helper's Name: _____   Date: _____

Teacher's Name: _____   Room Number: _____

Date	Book Title and Author	Follow-Up Skill Activities Review	Focus Standard

Notes _____

_____

_____

Extra Student Plan

From time to time, you may get an extra student in your class. This usually occurs when a teacher is absent and a substitute has not been obtained, so the absent teacher's class is usually broken up to various classrooms. This extra student can be in your room for a few minutes, a few hours, or a few days. If you find yourself in this situation, here are a few suggestions and ideas that can make having an extra student an easy adjustment.

- Have a routine that works when a student enters the room. Have a responsible student be the extra student's helper and guide. Have a place for the student to sit, a task for him or her to do, and extra work available.

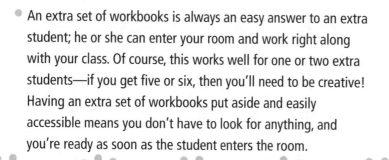

- An extra set of workbooks is always an easy answer to an extra student; he or she can enter your room and work right along with your class. Of course, this works well for one or two extra students—if you get five or six, then you'll need to be creative! Having an extra set of workbooks put aside and easily accessible means you don't have to look for anything, and you're ready as soon as the student enters the room.

- Workbooks enable a student to work along with your class. Another good idea besides the workbooks is a folder with worksheets that a student can keep and stay busy with. This folder should be in an easy place to access. The worksheets should be simple for the student to complete without much guidance from you, and they should be fun for the student. These folders can be premade and ready for any extra students you may get.

- At the beginning of the year, it's always helpful to save a few copies of everything your students have worked on, including extra workbooks, in case your extra student becomes permanent!

Sub Folder

A folder for a substitute teacher is good to have in case you are absent. This sub folder can be used by a sub whether your absence is planned or unexpected. If your absence is planned, then you may have more precisely detailed plans; nonetheless, a good sub folder is always an excellent resource. You should keep your sub folder in a place that's easy to find with simple directions for conducting class. Having a great sub folder will make life easier for your substitute, and your class can proceed as though you were present.

Sub Folder Cover
Your sub folder cover can benefit from a bright color that's easy to see. Bright yellow or gold is a great color!

First Page
This page is dedicated to the general information about the school, personnel, administration, etc.

Second Page
This page contains your daily class schedule. It is specific to your class and should be changed each year.

Third Page
This page contains your class seating chart.

Keep It Simple
Remember that, with a sub folder, less is more. A substitute is usually there for only a day or two. Make your plans clear and concise.

Activity Sheets
These pages should be activities that a sub can reproduce and use in case he or she has nothing to conduct class with. Use three different subject areas, i.e., Math, Language Arts, and Science. You may also include emergency plans and extra student referral forms.

Sub Feedback Form
This sheet is designed for a substitute to leave feedback to you as to how the day went. This sheet holds students accountable for their behavior, because they know that you will be getting feedback on how the day went.

General Information for Substitute

Welcome!

School: _____

Address: _____ Phone Number: _____

The Principal is: _____ The Vice Principal is: _____

The Counselor is: _____ and is located _____.

The Office Manager is: _____

The Custodial Person for this building is: _____

The Nurse is: _____ and is located _____.

School begins at _____ and dismisses at _____.

This general sheet is for room number _____ Mr./Mrs./Ms. _____ last updated

_____.

Two teachers who can be asked for help or answer any questions are: _____ room

number _____ and _____ room number _____.

The location this class will arrive for school is: _____.

The lunch area is located: _____.

The dismissal location for this class is: _____.

Two students who can assist you with class operations and general knowledge are:

_____ and _____.

My teacher's aide is _____ and arrives at _____.

Notes _____

_____

_____

_____

_____

Phone Extensions

Office: _____ Library: _____ Nurse: _____

Counselor: _____ Teacher #1: _____ Teacher #2: _____

Emergency: _____ Fire: _____ Police: _____

Other: _____ Other: _____ Other: _____

Sub Feedback Form

Name: _____   Employee Number: _____   Phone Number: _____

The Day

Things we accomplished:

Things we didn't get to:

The Class

Helpful hands:

Anecdotal

Concerns or Issues:

Name	Concern or Behavior	Action

Thanks for your help!

Seating Chart

Teacher: _____   School: _____

Year: _____   Room Number: _____

Classroom Map and Seating Chart

Notes, Special Needs, Etc.

Teacher Evaluation Environment Guide

Here are some recommendations of things you can be aware of within your room before being evaluated. Not all administrators are the same, and, depending on your administrator, these things might not carry as much weight. Regardless, it is nice to be able to check your room organization against this checklist and see how you're doing. This list shouldn't serve to make every room the exact same, but you can use this list to take you to a higher level in your teaching. It always helps to have ideas about what your administrator may be looking for, but hopefully he or she is paying more attention to your excellent teaching!

☐ Contents of students' desks neatly arranged

☐ Tops of student tables neat and clean

☐ Floors clean and free of paper debris

☐ Top of closets clear of clutter and boxes

☐ Students' coats and backpacks hung in closet

☐ Clean and neat closets

☐ Clean work tables

☐ Clean sink area

☐ Bookcases arranged neatly

☐ Class schedule posted

☐ Teacher's desk neat and organized

☐ Weekly lesson plan visible and on the desk

☐ Print-rich environment (charts and graphs)

☐ Furniture arrangement facilitates instruction

☐ Independent reading area

☐ Bulletin boards display students' work.

☐ Captions on boards promote critical thinking.

☐ Generally neat and clean learning environment.

☐ Teacher's name and teacher's aide name posted

☐ Emergency bag in easy location to access

Teacher Evaluation

ere is a list of *all* the areas that you will be expected to juggle in this profession. Remember, don't get overwhelmed, just do your best and keep adding to the list of things you're already doing. Good luck!!

Instructional Strategies

- Directed lessons
- Small vs. large group
- Use of different learning modalities
- Ongoing assessments
- Use of technology
- Student-driven activities

Record Keeping

- Student records up to date
- Student attendance accurately recorded
- Evidence of assessments
- Title I identification paperwork
- Referrals to the student success teams
- Any state paperwork completed
- Your credentials kept current

Parent/Guardian Involvement

- Home contact
- Parent volunteers
- Parent conferences
- Open house/back to school
- Parent workshops

Planning and Preparation

- Weekly plans w/objectives
- Long-range planning
- Planning for T.A.
- Appropriate curriculum
- Field trips, technology labs, etc.

Room Environment

- Evidence of standards
- Print-rich environment
- Great-looking bulletin boards
- Daily class schedule posted
- Clean and neat furniture

See Evaluation Checklist

Reminder

. . . .

Be strong and brave during your evaluation. An OK administrator will reprimand you if you need improvement, but a great administrator will help you get stronger in your weak areas. Don't be too hard on yourself; know that you're doing your best!

Classroom Management

- Students are on task.
- Clear expectations of student behavior
- Students follow directions.
- Students transition easily.
- Students are aware of standards.
- Students take responsibility.
- Good leadership

Professional and Adjunct Responsibilities

- Good attendance
- Attend staff meetings
- Extracurricular activities
- Attend professional development
- Neat and clean appearance
- Begin and end class on time
- Show leadership
- Evidence professional growth

Helpful Tips

. . . .

- Find a mentor teacher—a teacher who has been in the classroom for a while can be an excellent source of support and advice.
- Keep a portfolio of your work; this can be a great tool for personal growth!

Evaluation Checklist

Most districts have a formal evaluation process that is required every year to few years, depending on your status. New teachers are usually evaluated annually for the first few years. This can be a stressful event for even the most seasoned teacher. It is a good opportunity to focus on your room environment, planning, and teaching, and it can be a positive experience. The key here is to be prepared, organized, and focused on your lesson's objective.

☐ **Clean Room Environment**
A clean, inviting, child-centered room goes a long way and leaves a good impression, even when things are hectic.

☐ **Current Student Work Displayed**
Current bulletin boards are necessary. Try to rotate them, choosing a new board every two to three weeks. This way, they will stay current and aren't stressors. Check with your school for what needs to be displayed:

☐ Standards
☐ Open-ended question
☐ Board title
☐ Rubric
☐ Teacher comments
☐ Rubric score

☐ **Student Work Sample Folders**
- Collecting work samples is a good idea to keep as evidence of a student's performance.
- Some administrators will want to see them. Check with other teachers at your school.

☐ **Student Portfolio Box**
- Different from work samples (is a living collection that is updated by students)
- Collection of a select few work samples chosen by students (up to about ten)
- Check with other teachers for portfolio ideas.
- Keep a current collection of student work.

☐ **Current Lesson Plans**
- Keep up with weekly lesson plans!
- Ask other teachers how they plan.
- Check with your evaluating administrator on his or her expectations.

☐ **Long-Range Lesson Plan**
- It is a good idea to have long-range plans available.
- Some administrators may request them. Ask other teachers and your administrator.

☐ **Assessments**
- Assessments are very important, and most administrators will want to see evidence.
- Find out which district and/or school assessments are required. House them together.
- Find assessments that you are comfortable with for your own use.

☐ **Grade Book**
- Evidence of grades is very important and should also be available.
- Ask other teachers how they keep their grades, and find a system that works for you.

189

Tips for Back-to-School Night

This page is designed to assist you with back-to-school night. This sheet should serve only as suggestions for what you might want ready for the parents/guardians. Depending on your school or your own personal flair, your list may vary. A great idea is to discuss the areas listed below during the parent visitation.

Rubrics

These should be in plain view and easy to read. If you or your district doesn't use rubrics, this is a type of chart describing how you grade the academic performance of each student as well as assignments.

Literature

Back-to-school night gives parents/guardians a chance to see what types of books and texts their children are using. This display of books and texts will serve as a great way to not only reinforce what is being read in class but also provide parents/guardians with ideas of what to buy their child for their own home libraries!

Refreshments and Snacks

Using treats and refreshments at back-to-school night are a super way to begin any meeting. Everyone likes some type of snack, and eating makes people smile. When parents/guardians smile, that is a key to your success at back-to-school night.

Class Rules

Any great classroom has some type of class rules chart. There are many styles for this chart, but it should be very easy to understand and easy for students to follow.

Student Work or Portfolios

If possible, it's nice to have any current assessments and student work folders out on the desks and accessible to the parents/guardians. Parents/guardians will want to see how their child is doing so far. If time permits, you can have a more complete discussion with any parents/guardians you feel the need to talk to.

Educational Materials

All educational enhancements should be posted, and all your class bulletin boards should reflect the work being done in class. Think about an organized and colorful display that can really "wow" the parents and make you look great!

Class Expectations

A great way to start off the year is to explain exactly what you expect from the parents/guardians. A powerful way to reinforce this is to type out your expectations and give a copy to each parent. Getting off on the right foot with parents/guardians can save you a lot of time and can enhance their child's academic performance.

Activity or Learning Centers

Learning centers should be neat and clean. These centers will benefit from a label and instructions on how to use the materials. As with the books in the room, these centers provide a visual for the parents of what type of learning is going on in your classroom.

Back-to-School-Night Checklist

- ☐ Parent sign-in

- ☐ Snacks and juice

- ☐ Agenda (activities for the evening)

- ☐ Parent handouts (class expectations, homework policy, daily schedule, etc.)

- ☐ Name tags on desks

- ☐ Current bulletin boards (attractive with student work, schedule, etc.)

- ☐ Standards and rubrics on all bulletin boards

- ☐ Word wall

- ☐ Behavior standards and consequences posted

- ☐ Clean and orderly student and teacher desks

- ☐ Neat and tidy classroom

- ☐ Boxes stowed away

- ☐ Textbooks and learning materials displayed

- ☐ Student assessments and evaluations available

- ☐ Student portfolios (writing, assessments, math, etc.)

- ☐ High-quality student work samples

- ☐ Centers (labeled)

- ☐ Clean chalkboards

- ☐ Calendar with correct month and date

- ☐ Computers and software display

- ☐ Your own special touch

HELLO, PARENTS!

Date: _____

Dear Mr./Mrs./Ms. _____,

I would like to invite you to back-to-school night. I want to take just a few minutes to discuss expectations for the year, homework, and academic goals. Your attendance at this meeting would be greatly appreciated and extremely beneficial to your child's success! The date and time are _____.
See you then.

Thanks,

(Please fill out and return to school.)

✂ -

☐ Yes, I will be there!

☐ No, I can't make it.

Name: _____

Phone Number: _____

Student's Name: _____

Back-to-School Night Sign-in Sheet

Teacher: _____ Room Number: _____

Date: _____ Grade: _____ Time: _____

Date	Student's Name	Parent's Name	Comments

Parent Conference Reminders

The following is a list of reminders for you to consider during parent conferences. Parent conferences can be a great tool for you as the teacher. Parent conferences help you obtain additional information about the student from the parents. They allow you to share information with the parents/guardians about their child, discuss any concerns about the student, and, most importantly, enlist the cooperation of the parents/guardians in addressing the student's education.

- Try to establish a positive relationship with the parents/guardians before presenting any concerns.
- Allow the parents/guardians to talk.
- Avoid telling the parents/guardians what the student does not do in a negative way.
- Have your assessments, sample work, and report card ready to share with the parents/guardians.
- Avoid lecturing or talking down to the parents/guardians.
- Try to obtain the cooperation of the parents/guardians when dealing with the student's education.
- Do not use words with negative connotations, like *dumb, lazy, stupid,* or *bad.*
- Remember, be as positive with parents/guardians as possible. Parents/guardians can be a great asset to your educational program!

Conference Week Master Calendar

Time (_____ min.)	Monday Date: _____	Tuesday Date: _____	Wednesday Date: _____	Thursday Date: _____	Friday Date: _____
A.M.					
P.M.					

Teacher Reminders:

☐ Check with school for times and possible off-limit days.
☐ Fill in dates and times on template.
☐ Send home sign-up page.

☐ Assign conferences.
☐ Be prepared.
☐ Enjoy!

Conference Week Calendar

Dear Parent/Guardian:

We are scheduling conferences to meet and discuss your child's academic progress. Your child and I look forward to sharing all that we are learning in school. It is an important chance for all of us to get to know one another and to give your child recognition. I hope you can make it. To help me schedule you, please sign up for the most convenient times that you are available. Fill in your first, second, and third choices in the corresponding box and time, and I will do my best to accommodate you. I will send this schedule back with your child's name in the box of their assigned conference. Thank you for your support. I look forward to meeting you. Sincerely yours,

_____ Room Number _____

Time (_____ min.)	Monday Date: _____	Tuesday Date: _____	Wednesday Date: _____	Thursday Date: _____	Friday Date: _____
A.M.					
P.M.					

The Writing Process

Organizing your writing process can help facilitate your students' writing. Students can independently maintain an ongoing writing assignment while you assist individual students. The following is a way to organize your writing process and maintain a level of consistency. (*Note:* Upper-grade forms have different graphics.)

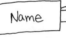

- Write or attach name.
- Create a tracking arrow.

- Glue posters together to create a long writing process poster.
- Track each student with clothespin.
- Helpful for conferencing—move clothespin once you have conferenced with student.

- Ongoing writing folder matches forms and posters.
- Students can move paper clip down the side to track where they are in the process.
- Folder houses papers from each phase.
- Use folder for the year—laminate it.

- Writing templates give consistency.
- Templates match posters.
- Have a supply of each form available.

197

Writing in Progress

Name:

Prewrite

Draft

Edit and Revise

Proofread

Publish

Share and Reflect

Prewrite

Draft

One day a dog went to
the pyk. He ran

Edit and Revise

Proofread

Publish

One day a dog went to the Park

Share and Reflect

Name: _____

Date: _____

Prewrite

Name: _____

Date: _____

Draft

☐ Edit and Revise   ☐ Proofread

Draft (continued)

☐ Edit and Revise   ☐ Proofread

Name: _____

Date: _____

Rubric Score ____ /____ /____ / = ____

Final Draft

Final Draft (continued)

Name: _____

Date: _____

My Story

_____

Writing in Progress

Name:

Prewrite

Draft

Edit and Revise

Proofread

Publish

Share and Reflect

Prewrite

Draft

Edit and Revise

Proofread

Publish

Name: _____

Date: _____

Prewrite

Name:

Date:

Draft

☐ **Edit and Revise**

☐ **Proofread**

Draft (continued)

☐ **Edit and Revise**

☐ **Proofread**

Name: _____

Date: _____

Final Draft

Rubric Score

___/___/___/ = ___

Final Draft (continued)

Name:

Date:

My Story

My Story (continued)

Bulletin-Board Checklist

Contents for a Great Bulletin Board

☐ Title (theme of the board)

☐ Students' work (with corrections, rubric score, and positive feedback)

☐ Open-ended question (extending their learning)

☐ Rubric (a rubric you develop identifying the criteria for the assignment)

☐ Standard (the standard you are teaching based on your state standards)

☐ Teacher work example (a model example for students to achieve)

Supplies to Complete the Board

Paper (colorful and fadeless, if possible)

Roll Paper (to back the board; chart paper if available)

Tag Board or Sentence Strips (for writing the question and standard)

Markers

Scissors

Stapler

Borders (make your own or buy from a local education supply store)

Students' Work

Tips for Superior Bulletin Boards

- Some administrators like all boards in the room to be the same colors.
- A great way to zest up your boards is to go for three colors instead of one.
- Mount students' work on two color sheets instead of one.
- Kid-friendly writing is always a brilliant idea.
- Boards should be consistent (questions and standards in the same place on each board).
- Try letting the students direct how the board should look.

Bulletin-Board Diagram

Rubric Score

Title or Theme

Border (two colors)

Student Work (double-mounted on colored paper)

Pictures or Added Artwork

Teacher-Created, Student-Friendly Rubric

Teacher Work Example

Open-Ended Question

State Standard

Fadeless Background Paper

Word Walls

Word walls can work for any student from kindergarten through twelfth grade. These word walls should contain words that are relevant to the work being done in your class. Word walls can go as far as your imagination can take them and can be put in several places in the classroom. As far as the word list itself, a good practice is to rotate your words at a consistent pace, not too fast and not too slow. Take your time and get a sense of what works best for your group of students. Every class is different, so what works one year may not work the following year. Word walls serve as a continuous reference point while the students master the words and definitions. Words posted on the wall or on a chart are a great way to make language fun, make words important, and get kids excited about learning vocabulary.

- Try to use the word wall frequently—the more you buy into the word wall, the more your students will buy in.
- Word walls can be an effective way to spotlight particular words that you want students to focus on.
- Not all words on the word wall have to be new; some words may repeat or stay up for a longer time.
- Have fun with this! Make it an easy and powerful way to enhance students' vocabulary.
- If possible, make the students responsible for changing and editing the list. Give your students ownership of the word wall!

- Use these sources:
  - Math vocabulary
  - Reading vocabulary
  - Sight words
  - Spelling words
  - Word families
  - Rhyming words
  - Thematic unit words
  - New vocabulary for curricular areas

- Not all words need to stay up for a long time; if the class has mastery of a word, then change it out for a new one.

227

Activities for Word Walls

1. Students can illustrate each word.

2. Use in daily oral activity—students can use the words in a sentence.

3. Put the words in *ABC* order.

4. Quiz the students on the words.

5. Define each word.

6. Discuss each word daily.

7. Have students create their own flash cards.

8. Use in a class recital or read-a-loud.

Placement Ideas for Word Walls

- Wall
- Chart Rack
- Chalkboard
- List Paper
- Journal Page
- Closet Door
- Bulletin Board
- Easel
- Label Room Items
- Other?

© The McGraw-Hill Companies, Inc.

Field-Trip Checklist

Trip: _____

Location: _____

Date: _____ **Time:** _____

Adults: _____

Six Weeks Prior
☐ Get permission from district—purpose, destination, and plan.
☐ Request transportation.

Two Weeks Prior
☐ Notify cafeteria
  ☐ sack lunches needed
  ☐ will purchase/provide (none needed)
  ☐ complete lunch request (if required).
☐ Confirm bus.
☐ Remind administrator.
☐ Letter home to notify parents of upcoming trip.*
☐ Invite any parent chaperones.
☐ Connect to theme or unit.

  Refer to school-trip policy.

Three Days Prior
☐ Send parental consents home.
  Leave in office (parent release)
  Take on Trip (student emergency contact)
☐ Prepare name tags.
☐ Discuss trip, safety, and procedures.

Trip Day
☐ Finalize count.
☐ Distribute name tags.
☐ Leave name list and consents in office, site information.
☐ Take parent and emergency contact information on each child.
☐ Use restroom.

☐ Assign trip buddies.
☐ Review trip procedures (times, restrooms, safety, etc.).
☐ Periodically take head count.

Follow-up
☐ Share, discuss, or write
  ☐ Write a story (favorite part, describe an attraction).
  ☐ Sequence the trip.
  ☐ Relate to theme.
  ☐ Compare and contrast what was seen.
  ☐ Draw a picture.
  ☐ Create a class mural.

Reflection and Notes: (What went well? What would you do differently? Etc.)

_____

_____

_____

_____

The following is a weekly checklist that can help you start your week. Add to the list. It is an excellent way to make sure you haven't forgotten anything.

Am I ready for the week?

☐ Lesson plans

☐ Attendance cards or roster

☐ Calendar

☐ Lesson materials: _____

_____

_____

☐ Spelling words

☐ Home study prepared

☐ Pencils sharpened

☐ Chalk or markers

☐ Paper

Week of: _____

☐ Art supplies: _____

_____

_____

☐ Trips or assemblies: _____

_____

_____

☐ Daily agenda

☐ Notices to go home

☐ _____

☐ _____

☐ _____

Am I ready for the week?

☐ Lesson plans

☐ Attendance cards or roster

☐ Calendar

☐ Lesson materials: _____

_____

_____

☐ Spelling words

☐ Home study prepared

☐ Pencils sharpened

☐ Chalk or markers

☐ Paper

Week of: _____

☐ Art supplies: _____

_____

_____

☐ Trips or assemblies: _____

_____

_____

☐ Daily agenda

☐ Notices to go home

☐ _____

☐ _____

☐ _____

Test-Taking Overview

Standardized tests are given in most school districts starting in first grade. Every district is different, and procedures vary from state to state. Check with your school to find out what tests are administered and when they are given. The following tips can assist in the preparation for and administration of tests. Follow your curriculum and standards as outlined by your district, and your students will be prepared. Start early in challenging them to be critical thinkers by giving them various opportunities to practice test taking. Standardized tests can be a stressful time for you and your students. The key is being ready.

Checklist:

☐ **Test guide booklet**

☐ **Test booklets**

☐ **Pencils (No. 2)**

☐ **Eraser(s)**

☐ **Scratch paper**

☐ **Student dividers**

☐ **Student markers**

☐ **Door sign**

☐ **Approved mathematical instruments**

Test-Taking Tips:

- Create dividers with chipboard and book-binding tape (every other student).

- Practice test taking; create multiple-choice assessments throughout the year (with bubbling in).

- Practice using scratch paper to transfer math problems for calculations (folding in half three times makes eight boxes).

- Provide students with markers to track problems (use a word card, construction paper, or index cards).

- Practice comprehension throughout the year. Write questions for anything read. Students can copy and answer—this teaches them to look back in the text for answers.

- Practice testing atmosphere whenever you are assessing to create a familiarity.

- Sit students where they will sit when taking test to familiarize them with their seating arrangement.

- Teach students to trust their first instinct.

- Teach students to quickly preview questions prior to reading a comprehension passage.

- Teach students to avoid stray marks on the actual test. All work must be done on scratch paper.

- Early finishers can read a book or draw on their scratch paper.

- Account for all testing materials daily (even scratch paper). You may have to actually sign them in and out.

- Take students to restroom prior to testing.

- Always have extra pencils and scrap paper ready.

- Know your students. Check to see if anyone requires special testing accommodations or has a parental exclusion signed.

- Make sure all tests are properly labeled and distributed. Account for all of them when finished.

- Always preview what you will test prior to administering the test. Be prepared!

- Get to know your proctor prior to testing. Establish a testing routine.

- Send a note home prior to testing that asks parents/guardians to have students at school on time, well rested, well fed, and dressed in comfortable clothing on the day of the test.

Lesson Planning

Unit-Plan Overview

his sheet is designed to help you plan for an entire unit. Using this sheet can be a great way for you to make sure that you cover major portions of the curriculum when doing a unit. An example is included below to show you what you should be including in your unit plan. This is just an example—feel free to change this, manipulate it, or create your own. This sheet can help you get those creative juices flowing when planning your unit.

- Be sure to include any specific literary sources and books that you may be using in this unit.

- Keep this with your weekly lesson plans as a guide to where you're going with your instruction as well as evidence of your planning. Your administrator will be happy to see this!

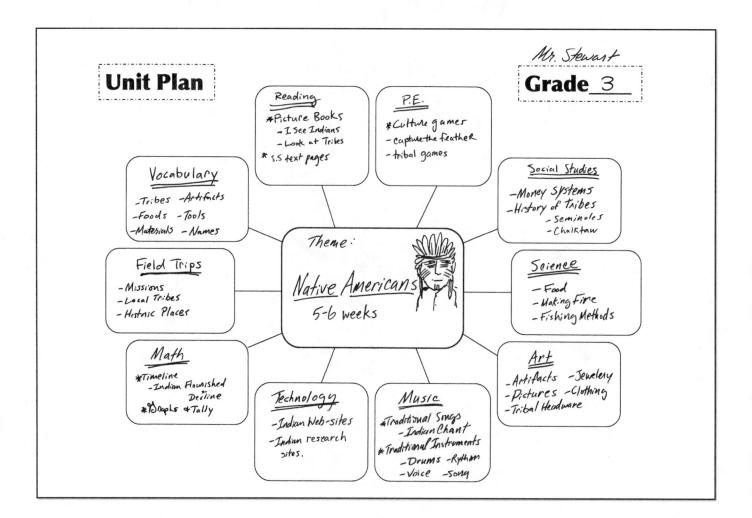

Teacher:
Grade:

Unit Plan

Direct-Instruction Lesson Plan

Title: _____ Unit: _____ Grade Level: _____

Teacher: _____ Suggested Time: _____

1. **Anticipatory Set and Scaffolding:**
   * Grab students' attention, then relate new objectives to past learning.

   Objective:

2. **Presentation and Procedure:**
   * List the sequential steps for the lesson you will model.

3. **Guided Practice:**
   * The students and teacher work together to carry out an example or activity to match the objective.

4. **Check for Understanding:**
   * Use a quick and simple assessment to confirm students' understanding.

5. **Independent Practice:**
   - Students work independently on a task that meets the objective.

6. **Assessment, Homework, or Project:**
   - Choose the method you will use to be sure students continue to understand the objective.

7. **Content Standards:**

8. **Modifications, Special Needs, or Technology Component:**

Lesson Plan

Title: _____ Unit: _____ Grade Level: _____

Teacher: _____ Suggested Time: _____

Instructional Objectives:

Materials and Equipment:

Vocabulary:

Anticipatory Set:

Input:

Lesson Steps:

Guided Practice:

Check for Understanding:

Independent Practice:

Closure:

Modifications, Special Notes, or Technology Component:

Assessment and/or Homework:

WEEKLY PLANNER Week	Morning Exercise	Phonics/ Spelling	Reading	Language Arts	Math	Science/Art/ P.E./S.S.	Homework
Monday							
Tuesday							
Wednesday							
Thursday							
Friday							

Home Study

Home study, or homework, is very important. It gives students a chance to practice and reinforce skills that have been covered in class. It also provides parents/guardians with an opportunity to take part in their child's education. Homework should be a review of skills covered that day and should be self-explanatory and focused. It is a strategic part of your planning. There are a number of activities that can be done without having to run off copies. The following are some suggestions.

Spelling-Word Template

- Fill out template and send home weekly.
- Supplement with any additional homework.

Name:

Weekly Spelling List

1. bake
2. rake
3. take
4. sail
5. pail
6. snail
7. shout
8. trout
9. sprout
10. bridge
11. ledge
12. badge
13. judge
14. their
15. there

Bonus

sailboat

Date:

Directions:
Complete daily assignments.
Return daily.

Monday:
- Write sentences with words 1-5.
- How many ways can you say 8?

Tuesday:
- Write sentences with words 6-10.
- How many ways can you say 9?

Wednesday:
- Write sentences with words 10-15.
- Write 3 story problems with the numbers 8 & 9.

Thursday:
- Put words in alphabetical order. Study words for test.
- How many ways can you say 10?

Friday:
- Write a story with as many words as you can.
- Write 3 story problems that equal 10.

© Springer/Alexander 2004

Math Activities

- Write problems to represent a number, "Ways to say a number."
- Create story problems.
- Write out fact families for a number.
- Count in various ways.

Spelling-Word Activities

- Write sentences with the words.
- Write synonyms or antonyms for the words.
- Alphabetize words.
- Write rhyming words.
- Illustrate the words.
- Write a paragraph with the words. Challenge students by giving them a title to use (e.g., "My Day at the Beach").
- Write a story using as many words as you can.

WEEKLY SPELLING LIST

1. _____

2. _____

3. _____

4. _____

5. _____

6. _____

7. _____

8. _____

9. _____

10. _____

BONUS _____

_____

Name: _____

Date: _____

DIRECTIONS: Complete daily assignments. Return daily.

MONDAY: _____

_____

_____

_____

TUESDAY: _____

_____

_____

_____

WEDNESDAY: _____

_____

_____

_____

THURSDAY: _____

_____

_____

_____

FRIDAY: _____

_____

_____

_____

WEEKLY SPELLING LIST

1. _____
2. _____
3. _____
4. _____
5. _____
6. _____
7. _____
8. _____
9. _____
10. _____
11. _____
12. _____
13. _____
14. _____
15. _____

BONUS
_____

Name: _____
Date: _____

DIRECTIONS: Complete daily assignments. Return daily.

MONDAY: _____
_____
_____
_____

TUESDAY: _____
_____
_____

WEDNESDAY: _____
_____
_____

THURSDAY: _____
_____
_____

FRIDAY: _____
_____
_____
_____

WEEKLY SPELLING LIST

1. _____
2. _____
3. _____
4. _____
5. _____
6. _____
7. _____
8. _____
9. _____
10. _____
11. _____
12. _____
13. _____
14. _____
15. _____
16. _____
17. _____
18. _____
19. _____
20. _____

Bonus

_____

Name: _____

Date: _____

DIRECTIONS: Complete daily assignments. Return daily.

Monday: _____
_____
_____
_____

Tuesday: _____
_____
_____
_____

Wednesday: _____
_____
_____
_____

Thursday: _____
_____
_____
_____

Friday: _____
_____
_____
_____

Portfolios

Student Assessment Portfolio Cover

Assessment folders can provide you with a strong way to track student performance and student growth as well as provide valuable information for report cards and grading. On the following page, you will find a portfolio cover sheet to place on your assessment folders. You may also want to enhance and create your own cover to fit your specific class needs. The cover below has been filled out as an example to show what one might look like. Use one folder per student. A nice touch is using the colored folders you can purchase at your local office supply store. Making a few extra blank folders will save you time if you get a new student during the year.

Write the name of your assessments here.

Student's name

Month the assessment is given in.

These boxes are to record your assessment scores. Assessments should be given three times a year (beginning, middle, and end).

Year

Student Alexander, London   **Year** 2006-07

Assessments

	Sept.	Dec	May	Growth Totals	
				Sept. - Dec.	Dec.- May
Phonics	91/200	124/200		33	
Oral Reading	2A	3		1	
High Frequency Words	87/100	92/100		5	
Totals (3 assessments)	180	219		39 +	

	10 wds.	20 wds.	30 wds	40 wds		
Reading	1 min ✓	1 min ✓				

Math Assessments	Sept. 75/100	Dec 88/100	May

Total points achieved (for all assessments)

Math assessment scores

Extra boxes (for other assessments or district-required information)

This sheet can be glued on a colored folder for that extra touch!

Growth totals (beginning-middle and middle-end)

STUDENT: _____

YEAR: _____

ASSESSMENTS

GROWTH TOTALS

MONTH/DATE

MONTH/DATE

MONTH/DATE

PHONICS

ORAL READING

HIGH-FREQUENCY WORDS

TOTALS (THREE ASSESSMENTS)

MATH ASSESSMENTS

WRITING PORTFOLIO
BEGINNER

STUDENT'S NAME: _____

ROOM: _____ TEACHER: _____

WRITING ASSESSMENTS

DATE

TOPIC/GENRE

UNIT NARRATIVES

DATE

THEME/PROMPT

FRIENDLY LETTER

DATE

PURPOSE

STRATEGIES:

CONVENTIONS:

WRITING PORTFOLIO

INTERMEDIATE

STUDENT'S NAME:

ROOM: _____ TEACHER:

WRITING ASSESSMENTS

DATE

TOPIC/GENRE

UNIT NARRATIVES

DATE

THEME/PROMPT

FRIENDLY LETTER (date, salutation, body, closing, and signature)

DATE

PURPOSE

STRATEGIES:

CONVENTIONS:

EXPOSITORY

DATE

SOURCE

WRITING PORTFOLIO

ADVANCED

STUDENT'S NAME:

ROOM: _____ TEACHER: _____

UNIT WRITING ASSESSMENTS

DATE

TOPIC/GENRE

NARRATIVE

DATE

THEME/PROMPT

DESCRIPTIVE

RESPONSE TO LITERATURE

DATE

PERSUASIVE

LETTER

DATE

PURPOSE

RESEARCH/EXPOSITORY

DATE

SOURCE

STRATEGIES:

CONVENTIONS:

STUDENT'S NAME: _____

ROOM: _____ TEACHER: _____

MATH PORTFOLIO

NUMBER SENSE
(counting, adding to 20, comparing values, <, >, =, the value of coins, ones and tens)

(WEEK 6)	(WEEK 12)	(WEEK 18)	(WEEK 24)	(WEEK 30)	(WEEK 36)

ALGEBRA AND FUNCTIONS
(number sentences, =, +, −, adding and subtracting)

MEASUREMENT AND GEOMETRY
(length, weight, time, shapes, planes and solids, directions)

STATISTICS, DATA ANALYSIS, AND PROBABILITY
(sorting, comparing, graphs, patterns, tally charts)

MATHEMATICAL REASONING
(using tools [e.g., a ruler], sketches, justifying, making decisions on problems)

Assessments

Assessments

Assessments are an integral part of your instructional program. They allow you to know where your students are with a skill and what gains they have made. Many districts or schools have set assessments and/or use curricular assessments to evaluate their students. These are very important; however, there are times when you may need to assess students on a specific skill or skills. There are many excellent assessment resources available, and you should ask other teachers what they use. Then you can try a few of them and find out which ones work for you. Keep assessments short and focused. The following are templates that can be used to create your own assessments. Use your school's designated curriculum to create tailored assessments.

Math Assessment — Name: _____ Date: _____
Focus: double digit +/−

1. 37 +43	2. 65 − 37
3. 87 −35	4. 31 +19
5. 23 +80	6. 97 − 39
7. 40 −17	8. 63 +17

Score: ____/____ Observation: _____
© Springer/Alexander 2004

Math Assessment

- Select up to eight math problems.
- Focus on a particular skill or standard.

Sight Word Assessment — Name: _____ Date: _____

the	no	this
a	was	said
is	here	of
on	an	my
are	too	do
you	says	does
see	can	we
have	like	they
but	with	where
she	it	were

Score: ____/____ Observation: _____
© Springer/Alexander 2004

Sight-Word Assessment

- Write in targeted sight words.
- Students can read and be scored on the correct number read.

Reading Assessment — Name: _____ Date: _____
Focus: short vowels /sight words

The Cat
One day a cat went to the park. — 2, 10
He saw his friends the bird and the dog. — 19
They played in the sun. They napped under — 27
a tree. After their nap they ate a — 35
snack. They ate chips and drank milk. — 42
They were full. It was late so they — 50
said good bye and went home. It was — 58
a good day. They were happy. They will — 66
play again. — 68

Observations: _____
Time: _____
© Springer/Alexander 2004

Reading Assessment

- Write or photocopy a passage or write sentences.
- Target specific spelling patterns or level.
- Students can be timed (e.g., one minute) to see how many words they can read in a designated time period (fluency).
- Students can be timed as they read a passage.
- Number words per line for ease of scoring.

Subject Assessment — Name: _____ Date: _____
Focus: Science ~ Life

Six things I learned about:

Topic

Standards Covered:
✓ 2.b Sequential stages of life cycles for different animals.
✓ 2.c Characteristics are inherited from parents.
✓ 2.d Variation among individuals of one kind.

Rubric Score: ____/____/____ = ____
© Springer/Alexander 2004

Subject Assessment

- Social Science or Science
- Students write up to six things they have learned about a topic.
- List the standards covered.

Dictation Assessment — Name: _____ Date: _____

Word dictation:
1. _____
2. _____
3. _____

Sentence dictation:
1. _____
2. _____
3. _____

Score: Word dictation: ____/____ Observation: _____
Sentence dictation: ____/____ Observation: _____
© Springer/Alexander 2004

Dictation Assessment

- Target specific spelling patterns.
- Dictate words and sentences.
- Score the assessment.

Name: _____ Date: _____

FOCUS: _____

1.	2.
3.	4.
5.	6.
7.	8.

Score: _____ / _____   Observations: _____

Name: _____ Date: _____

Score: _____ / _____   Observations:

Name: _____ Date: _____

FOCUS:

_____
_____
_____
_____
_____
_____
_____
_____
_____
_____
_____
_____
_____
_____
_____
_____
_____
_____

Time: _____ Observations:

Name: .... Date: ....

FOCUS:

SIX THINGS I LEARNED ABOUT _____

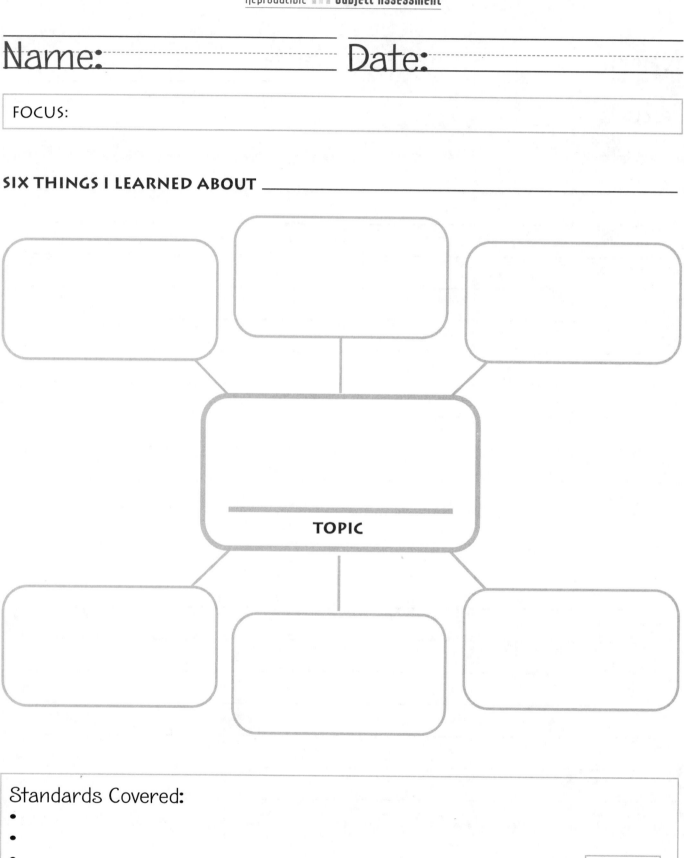

TOPIC

Standards Covered:
-
-
-

Rubric Score: _____ / _____ / _____ = [   ]

DICTATION ASSESSMENT

Name:

Date:

WORD DICTATION:

1.

2.

3.

4.

5.

6.

7.

8.

9.

SENTENCE DICTATION:

1.

2.

3.

Score: Word dictation: _____ / _____ Observation:

Sentence dictation: _____ / _____ Observation:

Rubrics

Rubrics are an excellent way to score your students' work. Generally, you can select three to five specific goals or targeted skills that you want an assignment to reflect. Your students are then scored on a scale of 1–4 based on their level of achievement for each skill. This can be as easy as a verbal explanation and circulating around the room marking student assignments as a 1, 2, 3, or 4. It can also be in the form of a written rubric that is posted on a bulletin board or other prominent area in the classroom. It is very important to have clear expectations so that students understand what they specifically need to achieve for a set score or you are able to explain why they received a set score.

4
- "Ultimate Goals"
- Three to five goals
- Explicit

3
- "Most Goals"
- Excellent attempt—needs a few minor corrections
- Use words like *most, no more than two mistakes.*

2
- "Some Goals"
- Attempted but needs support
- Use words like *some, three to four errors* (in regard to goal)

1
- "Minimal Goals"
- Minimal attempt, needs a great deal of support
- Use words like *no/little evidence of, minimal, more than five errors*

- Goals should be limited from three to five in an assignment.
- Goals should be explicit and specific.
- Goals need to be verbally communicated and explained to students.

- Graphics like smiley faces are helpful with primary students. Instead of a sad face, use a neutral one for "1," because a student shouldn't feel like an attempt is "sad" but rather that he or she needs support.

Example:

Goal: To have students use correct ending punctuation.

4   *All* sentences have the correct ending punctuation.

3   *Most* of the sentences have the correct ending punctuation (no more than two errors).

2   *Some* of the sentences have correct ending punctuation (no more than three to four errors).

1   There is *little to no evidence* of ending punctuation (more than five errors).

Demonstration Rubrics

You can create a demonstration rubric to illustrate how a rubric works and make them easier to understand. The following are three examples.

Hamburger Rubric

4
- Hamburger
- Bun
- Ketchup and mustard
- Lettuce and tomato

3
- Hamburger
- Bun
- Ketchup and mustard

2
- Hamburger
- Bun

1
- Hamburger

Pizza Rubric

4
- Pepperoni
- Mushrooms
- Cheese
- Tomato sauce

3
- Mushrooms
- Cheese
- Tomato sauce

2
- Cheese
- Tomato sauce

1
- Tomato sauce

4 Perfect score, can't ask for more. Look at me, I am a four!

3 Almost perfect, look at me. Doing great, I am a three.

2 Still much to do, makes me a two. But I can do it, I'll show you.

1 I have just begun. With hard work, I'll get it done, but for now I'm just a one.

What's my rubric score: 1, 2, 3, or 4?

- You can make these into posters.
  - Use construction paper for the hamburger.
  - Use a paper plate for the pizza, construction paper, yellow yarn for cheese.

Sample Writing Rubric

Assignment: Write a one-paragraph personal narrative about your most memorable or a favorite time you had with a friend.

Include: The name of your friend, when and where the experience occurred, and why it was memorable. Be sure to write neatly and use correct punctuation, capitalization, and spelling. Also use descriptive words in your writing.

A specific number range is helpful if you are heavily targeting a skill. Words like *few*, *several*, or *many* allow you flexibility if you don't want as much emphasis on an area.

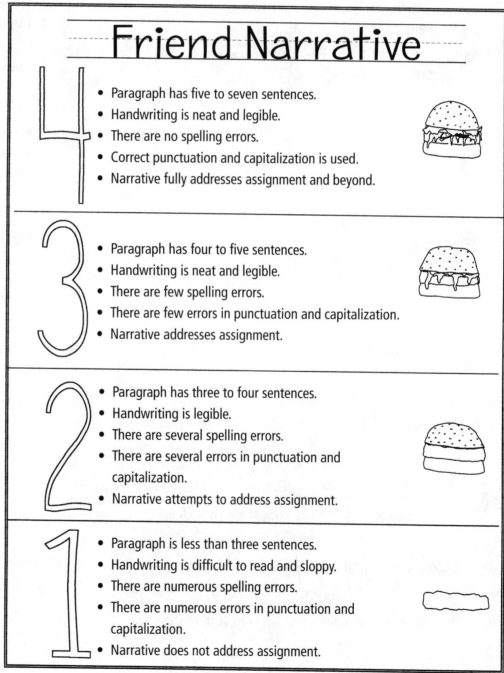

Friend Narrative

4
- Paragraph has five to seven sentences.
- Handwriting is neat and legible.
- There are no spelling errors.
- Correct punctuation and capitalization is used.
- Narrative fully addresses assignment and beyond.

3
- Paragraph has four to five sentences.
- Handwriting is neat and legible.
- There are few spelling errors.
- There are few errors in punctuation and capitalization.
- Narrative addresses assignment.

2
- Paragraph has three to four sentences.
- Handwriting is legible.
- There are several spelling errors.
- There are several errors in punctuation and capitalization.
- Narrative attempts to address assignment.

1
- Paragraph is less than three sentences.
- Handwriting is difficult to read and sloppy.
- There are numerous spelling errors.
- There are numerous errors in punctuation and capitalization.
- Narrative does not address assignment.

Sample Math Rubric

Assignment: Draw and solve a mathematical story problem.

Include: Illustrate the story problem clearly, showing how it can be solved mathematically. Write a sentence telling how the problem was solved.

Math may have fewer criteria in the rubric. Use standards to target specific skills.

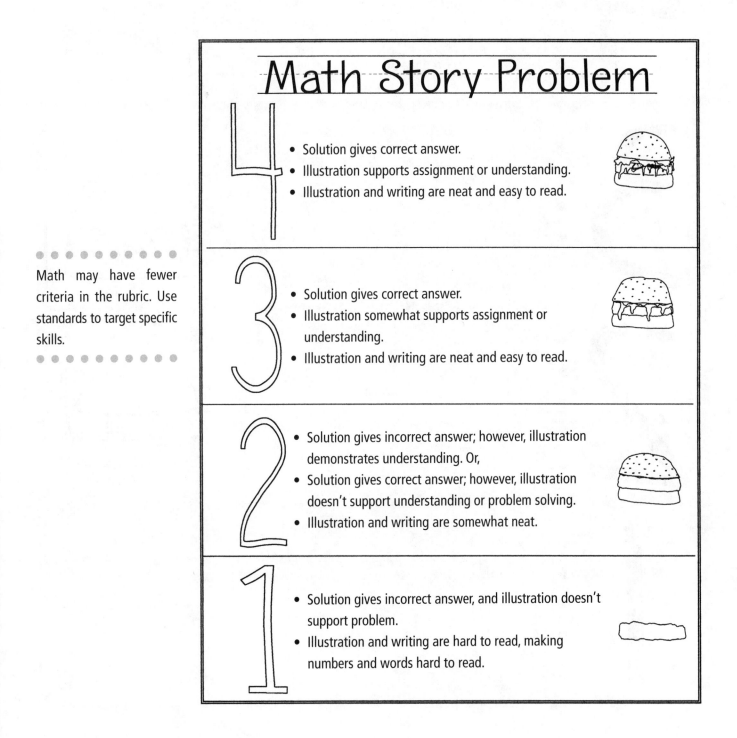

Math Story Problem

4
- Solution gives correct answer.
- Illustration supports assignment or understanding.
- Illustration and writing are neat and easy to read.

3
- Solution gives correct answer.
- Illustration somewhat supports assignment or understanding.
- Illustration and writing are neat and easy to read.

2
- Solution gives incorrect answer; however, illustration demonstrates understanding. Or,
- Solution gives correct answer; however, illustration doesn't support understanding or problem solving.
- Illustration and writing are somewhat neat.

1
- Solution gives incorrect answer, and illustration doesn't support problem.
- Illustration and writing are hard to read, making numbers and words hard to read.

Name:

4

3

2

1

Name:

4 :

3 :

2 :

1 :

Name:

4

3

2

1

Name:

4

3

2

1

Name:

4

3

2

1

Student Skills Review Sheet

The following page contains sheets that you can use with your teacher's aide to focus on low-achieving students or students who may just need some review. You may want to design a sheet that will fit your particular program. Use these sheets as a starting place, then create your own. These practical sheets will give you a focus for your teacher's aide and will support your in-class instruction.

- List of students needing review
- Your aide can put a check mark after each time he or she has worked with a student.
- Name of month and the date
- Insert the codes of the skills that each student needs to review.

Student List for Skills Review

STUDENTS	July																			SKILLS
	1	4	5	6	7	8	11	12	13	14	15	18	19	20	21	22	25	26	27	28	
Kacee	✓+	✓+	✓-	✓+	✓+	✓+															ABS
James	✓+	✓+	✓+	✓-	✓+	✓+															ABS
Xena	✓-	✓+	✓+	✓+	✓+																BSD
Willy	✓+	✓+	✓+	(Ab)	✓+																BSD
Kashala	✓+	✓+	✓+	✓+	✓+																SDR

Notes
* Kacee needs more work on her CVC blending. (faster blending phonemes)

* Willy is close to dipthong & sight word mastery.

Key
A = alphabet
B = CVC words
S = sight words
D = dipthongs
R = reading

- You may want to assign a time limit to each student.
- Your aide can write notes about particular students and their progress.
- Enter the particular review skills with a corresponding code.

- Each month, you can evaluate your students' progress and make changes according to their growth.
- All students on the list should be seen daily.
- This sheet should be put in a folder along with the review material for your aide.

271

Student List for Skills Review

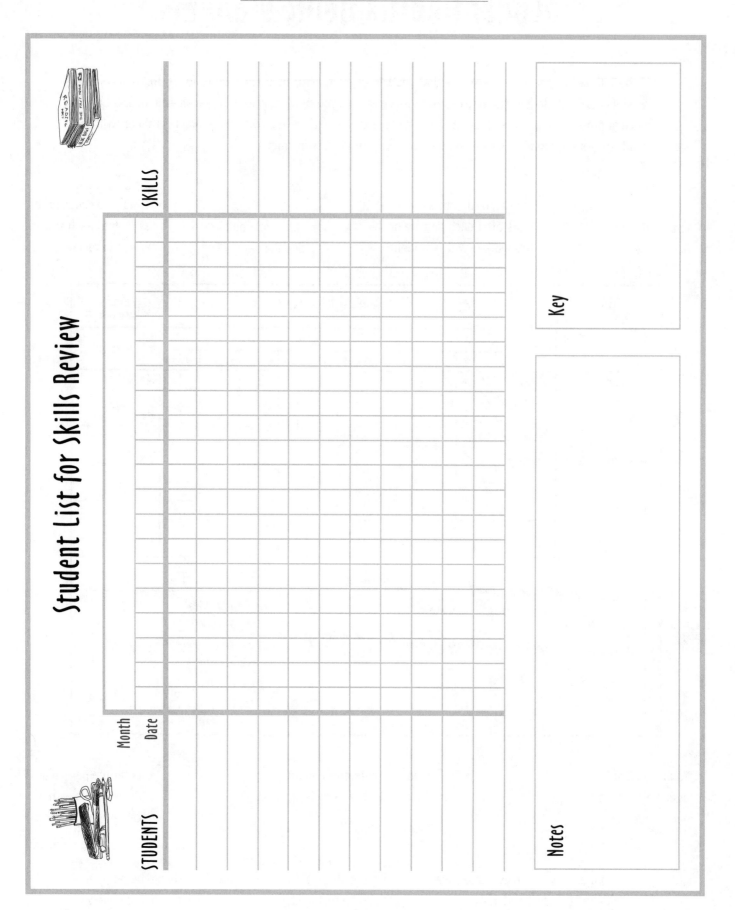

SKILLS

STUDENTS

Month

Date

Key

Notes

Weekly Assessment Overview

This is an assessment that can be given weekly in your class. This weekly assessment can help you to track your student's progress. This assessment is two sided, with one side having spelling and behavior and the other side having a simple math assessment that you can create. Both of these reproducible assessments are found on the following pages. It's a great idea to keep track of these scores on a grade sheet and have it available for conferences or administrators. Send this assessment home every Friday as a way to give parents/guardians feedback on their child's behavior for the week as well as their child's scores on the spelling and math assessments.

- Spelling test with the score
- Spelling and math scores
- Behavior chart with the appropriate boxes checked
- Choose problems that reflect what the students have learned for the week.
- Math score

FRONT

BACK

- Two practice sentences with corrections made
- A note to the parents/guardians
- Parent's signature
- Math test that you create and grade (can be formatted to be like your state test)

Name:

WEEKLY SPELLING TEST

1.

2.

3.

4.

5.

6.

7.

8.

9.

10.

Date:

BEHAVIOR

	😀	😟
Attendance (asistencia)	☐	☐
Classroom Behavior (comportamiento en la clase)	☐	☐
Yard Behavior (comportamiento en la yarda)	☐	☐
Homework (tarea)	☐	☐
Work Quality (cualidad de trabajo)	☐	☐
Spelling (deletreo) %	☐	☐
Math (matemática) %	☐	☐

Comments (comentario)

Parent's Signature (firma del padre)

SENTENCE

Name: _____

Date: _____

WEEKLY SPELLING TEST

1. _____
2. _____
3. _____
4. _____
5. _____
6. _____
7. _____
8. _____
9. _____
10. _____
11. _____
12. _____
13. _____
14. _____
15. _____
16. _____
17. _____
18. _____
19. _____
20. _____

BEHAVIOR

	🙂	🙁
Attendance (asistencia)	☐	☐
Classroom Behavior (comportamiento en la clase)	☐	☐
Yard Behavior (comportamiento en la yarda)	☐	☐
Homework (tarea)	☐	☐
Work Quality (cualidad de trabajo)	☐	☐
Spelling (deletreo) _____%	☐	☐
Math (matemática) _____%	☐	☐

Comments (comentario)

_____

_____

_____

_____

_____

Parent's Signature (firma del padre)

_____

Sentences

_____

_____

Name: _____ Score: _____ %

1.	2.
3.	4.
5.	6.
7.	8.
9.	10.

Weekly Assessment Grade Sheet

M = Math
S = Spelling

STUDENTS

Date

	M	S	M	S	M	S	M	S	M	S	M	S	M	S	M	S	M	S	M	S	M	S	M	S	M	S	M	S	M	S

Weekly Assessment Grade Sheet

M = Math
S = Spelling

Date

STUDENTS

	M	S	M	S	M	S	M	S	M	S	M	S	M	S	M	S	M	S	M	S	M	S	M	S	M	S

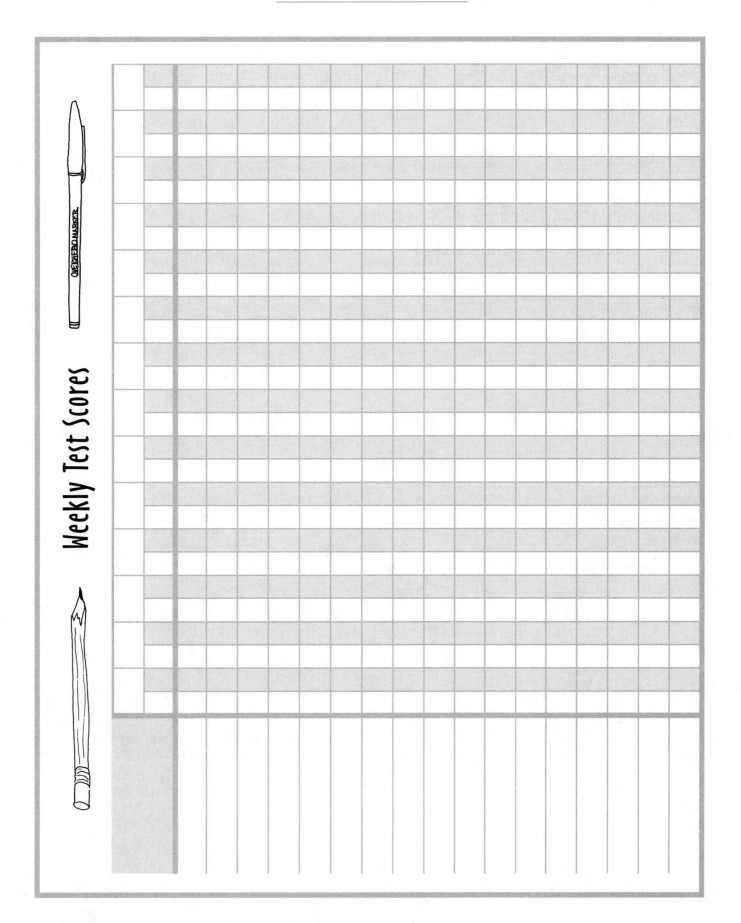

Weekly Test Scores

Meet the Authors

This book is a winning combination of practical, creative strategies and is the perfect resource whether you are seeking or continuing your career in education. It was created by two teachers who are artists and right-brain thinkers and who have been using these skills in their classrooms for many years. As mentors and master teachers, Steve Springer and Brandy Alexander have spent years perfecting their craft. They have become valuable resources to others in the field with their workbooks, posters, and practical activity sheets that are tailored to the specific needs of follow-up, assessment, and record keeping. These two have an innate ability to see the bigger picture and apply this vision specifically to the needs of a diverse student population. The classroom is an ever-changing environment, and being teachers in the field helps Steve and Brandy keep their focus on the current demands. Along the same lines, they realize the importance of clean, easy-to-follow, practical resources without a lot of extra baggage. Too many times, good material is wasted because it holds too much, becoming overwhelming, and is thus discarded on the teacher's shelf. This team knows what is going on. They are there day in and day out and want to make a difference.

Steve Springer served in the Peace Corps in Guatemala from 1988 to 1991. He ran 4-H clubs under the Ministry of Agriculture in Guatemala. He developed and implemented training for other volunteers as well as for host-country nationals. He has taught in the Los Angeles School District for twelve years. For two of those years, he worked with the district reading program, where he helped develop and serve as the director of a cross-aged tutoring program. He went on to help develop other after-school tutoring and phonics-based intervention programs. Steve returned to the classroom in 2002, where he is currently teaching and has served as a mentor and master teacher. His practical approach and ability to design hands-on, practical materials for the classroom have earned him recognition.

Brandy Alexander recently completed his Masters of Fine Arts from California State University, Los Angeles. Brandy continues to work primarily in ceramics and has shown his sculptures on the West Coast. Prior to that, he received his teaching credential from California State University and received the Golden Apple award from his class for excellence in the program. Brandy has been teaching for eight years. He has been a leader at his school, serving as grade-level chair and track coordinator. He has served as director of the Arts Prototype Grant for the past three years, implementing the program, overseeing the budget, and writing grants. He has served as a master and mentor teacher, sharing his practical approach and materials.

Steve and Brandy recognize the need for classroom materials that offer real learning opportunities and follow-up. Using their creative talent and teaching know-how, they have created a collection of teacher materials that will support you and give you an immediate, usable resource. As mentor and master teachers, they have seen a tremendous need for packaging the critical structure

281

and organization components that only come with years of experience. If you are a new teacher, you may be overwhelmed with everything from setting up your classroom to the daily management of a classroom. While you have had bits and pieces of these elements over your years of preparation and studies, you have not had a resource available that pulls it all together in one place. What better resource than one created by teachers in the field, teachers who have a creative edge and offer years of their own experience? It saves time and gives you only what you need.

Kimberly Persiani-Becker, Ed.D., Assistant Professor for Curriculum and Instruction at California State University, Los Angeles, served as the academic advisor and coauthor for this book. She has been an advocate for new teachers and children for several years. Most of her efforts have been focused on children and new teachers in urban school settings and from diverse backgrounds. Having taught at two other universities, she has been privileged to teach several classes in Teacher Education. Kimberly's personal education and experience gears her to teach within urban school settings, and her interests lie within the parameters of equity in education and cultural diversity. She currently teaches courses in classroom management for the elementary and early-childhood classrooms, and her students have requested many of the aids from this book. Additionally, she supervises student teachers during their directed teaching experience. She met Steve and Brandy as they were serving as master teachers for her students. During the 2003–2004 academic school year, Kimberly's contact with Steve and Brandy developed into an ongoing discussion of the practices they were implementing in their classrooms and the positive effects these practices were having on her student teachers. This prompted the notion of getting these practices published. With her experience and guidance, the three began the process of compiling their best strategies and techniques, which has resulted in this book.